Forgive Us Our Trespasses

A PLAYWRIGHT BY
MYRA L. TURNAGE

FULL CIRCLE PUBLISHING
BILOXI, MS

Full Circle Publishing
PO Box 8549
Biloxi, MS 39535

The following is a play and a work of fiction and any names, characters, places, and/or incidents are the product of the author's imagination and own resources. Any resemblance to persons, living or dead, is entirely coincidental; however, much of this story is based on actual events in the life of the author and her brother.

For information address Full Circle Publishing Rights Department, PO Box 8549, Biloxi, MS 39535

Editing by Full Circle Publishing & Julie Keene
Manufactured in the United States of America

ISBN-13: 978-0692904992 (Full Circle Publishing)
ISBN-10: 0692904999

www.juliekeene.com

~

I dedicate this playwright to my dearest brother   Willie.
Not only did we share the exact same birthday three years
apart but we both shared the love of adventure and
exploration of things mystical.   Willie so like many of us
was always in the pursuit of happiness. I know he has
found that in Heavenly places where our earthly beings
cannot comprehend but only imagine as we press toward
the promise of our Heavenly Father.   Willie because of
you I had the courage to finally put down on paper the
imagination that you so inspired in me. I will always be
grateful to have known you my big brother. Willie your
love lives on in the hearts of those who had the honor to
know you.

~

FORGIVE US OUR TRESPASSES

Makayla: *A young urban diva currently working as a paralegal. She is putting in part-time hours towards getting her law degree. Her pastime passion is collecting antiques and interior decorating. That's Makayla.*

Makyle: *(Makayla's twin brother is a railroad worker and broker who enjoys small town living and anything that has to do with nature and wildlife).*

Makayla: *(Struggles to find her cell phone in the dark, since only a few have her cell number, she answers)* This better be good, it's 5am.

Makyle: Fish are biting at 5 AM...and a cold one. *(Laying back with his feet propped. Reel cast into the waters of his favorite lake, continued with...)* Love you too sis.

Makayla: Did you have to love me so early? Or could this have waited at least till noon?

Makyle: Well since I have your attention, there's something I want you to check out! Freddie B and I.

Makayla: Freddie B? Tell him I said hello.

Freddie B: (*A local sheriff and best friend of Makyle who never quite got over his childhood crush on Makayla takes over the phone conversation and puts the phone on speaker.*) It sure would be nice to see that sweet face of yours.

Makayla: Oh! Freddie B. hi! Sure! Maybe next time I am in that neck of the woods.

Freddie B: Promise?

Makayla: Well, you know the last time we made promises to each other, someone ended up with a face full of tears.

Makyle: Ok you two love birds.

Freddie B: Sweetie let's talk later. (*Takes Makayla off speaker*)

Makyle: As I was saying, Freddie B. and I came across an old abandoned house in the middle of the woods. I mean a treasure chest literally.

Makayla: Ok!

Makyle: Really, this house was full of antiques.

Makayla: Antiques!!

Makyle: Yeah, I thought that might get your attention

Makayla: Antiques!

Makyle: Crystal, clothes, costume jewelry, furniture. It's literally a treasure chest.

Makayla: And you say this house is abandoned?

Makyle: Sure, had it checked out and everything.

Makayla: I hope so, you know you are in the SIP and they don't play. Just want to make sure everything is on the up and up.

Makyle: Like I said, It checks out. Besides, you know Freddie B. is the man around here. The house wasn't boarded up. There were no "No Trespassing" signs. It appeared to be abandoned and I mean a long time ago. I even came across a newspaper from 1954.

Makayla: Over 40 years ago!

Makyle: How long the belongings had been in this house or how long it's been since anyone resided here, I haven't a clue.

Makayla: Interesting! So? What do you want me to check out?

Makyle: There was this one piece that I think might be worth something. Your dealings with antiques and Big Wigs might come in handy.

Makayla: You know, I'd really love to help you out any way I can. I'll show you some love maybe!

Makyle: Ok, so I'll be at Hartsfield Jackson on Tuesday and I'll call you back later with my flight information.

Makyle: Hey, gotta go! Got a bite!

Makayla: Yea right! I love you. *(Makyle and Freddie B lean back and each sip on a cold one)*

Meanwhile, Makayla decides she might as well get out of bed and go for an early morning run.   She jumps into her sweats and pops on her head set and heads out the door. She thinks to herself, how beautiful Decatur is in early Fall.

Makayla: Love this weather (*She does a couple of miles then heads back to her favorite place - Dekalb Farmers Market. Walking through the front door she answers her cell phone*) Hi Jaden!

Makayla: You know me-Up! Besides, Kyle woke me up a couple of hours ago. Can you believe, at 4:00 am SIP time, he's on the banks rared back putting down a cold one.

Jaden: Ah! Can you do that in English? (*They both laugh*)

Makayla: The fruit and vegetables here are awesome. I love! I love! (*Makayla kisses a beautiful red apple, drops it into her basket and selects several more*).

Jaden: So, how's your brother?

Makayla: Fine. He'll be in for a visit day after tomorrow.

Jaden: Really! So I'll finally get to meet big brother?

Makayla: I certainly hope so. I have someone on the other line, can I hit you back? I'm sure it's mom.

Jaden: Take care.

Makayla: Hi Mom! So you heard Kyle would be coming down day after tomorrow. Oh, you did now?

Makayla finishes her shopping at the Farmers Market and heads home

Later that evening on the phone, Makayla informs Jaden that she spent the last three hours at Hopewell).

Makayla: With Pastor you don't just leave, you want to stay for the whole service, but now I'm taking a nap, I've been up since 0500.

Later, about 7:00pm Makayla goes into the shower, and gets ready for her date. The doorbell rings. In walks Mark. They embrace, sit for a while sharing some good conversation. Then they enjoy a nice candle-lit dinner that Makayla prepared. After dinner, low lights, soft music and lots of sweet nothings and dancing. Makayla keeping in the back of her mind that she is going to take this one real slow.

Makayla: I've really enjoyed your company.

Mark: I hate to leave.

Makayla: Me too.

Mark: Goodnight sweet.

Makayla blows out the candles, goes straight to her bedroom undress and falls asleep. The next morning Makayla sleeps in late 10am. 10am, yea that's late for Makayla. Finally she gets up goes for a morning run, returns home and dresses for shopping. Shortly she ends up at Home Depot and begins excitedly comparing paint samples and fabric swatches. She finds herself there for at least 2.5 hours.

After her long but enjoyable evening at Home Depot, she decides to swing by the Linen Loft. She picks up a few things to spruce up the spare bedroom for Ky's arrival tomorrow - new sheets and scented candles.

Makayla: My baby brother, how spoiled you are. New sheets and gardenia and lavender scented candles and fragrances. And I must not forget matches just in case you want to light up the candles. My brother-his rough outdoorsy side sure gets a kick out of me spoiling him.

Makayla: And the fridge is stocked.

Makayla goes home, puts away her shopping. She is about to enjoy a little meal when the doorbell rings. It's hand delivered red roses, a dozen and from no one other than Mark. A card that says "I loved our last evening together, can't wait to see you again". Along with the roses was a Maxwell CD. Makayla puts the roses in water and enjoys her meal.

Makayla: (*Smiling and thinking out loud*) I like.

Makayla decides to put on some shorts and a Tee and treats herself to a well-deserved pedi while watching a few flicks. Tonight just happens to be a Sidney Poitier

marathon. As she finishes up, they call me Mr. Pibbs,
she cleans up her mess, heads to the bedroom, turns off
the lights, pops in Maxwell, and falls asleep to
Fortunate.

THE NEXT DAY

After finishing up a few things around town and
putting together her luggage for a New York trip she
has later in the month, she heads to the airport.

A patient Makyle is standing at carousel C watching out
for luggage when he hears a familiar voice.

Makayla: Where have you been all my life?

He turns around and is greeted by the most beautiful
face and smile. He hugs and literally lifts his sister off
the floor.

Makyle: Woman, you know you look more and more
like mom each time I see you.

Makayla: And brother you *(she slaps him on the*
shoulder) are looking good yourself!

Makyle flings his duffle bag over his shoulder as they
head for the door.

Makayla: Yea, let's head for I-20 East so we can get well ahead of traffic.

Makyle: Sis, it is only 2pm.

Makayla: And your point might be? *(They both laugh and head up I-20 and make a right on Panola Road.)*

Makyle: I don't remember your place being so far out.

Makayla: Oh, I'm swinging by my girlfriend's house to drop off something for my Godson. I picked up an outfit at the mall this weekend. Can't wait another day to give it to him. *(Shortly she pulls up at the driveway).*

Makayla: I'll be right back. *(Then, she disappears inside. Only after a few minutes she returns).*

Jaden, standing in the doorway, waves goodbye to her friend.

Makyle: *(With a pleased look on his face)* They sure don't make housewives the way they used to.

Makayla: I suppose not! But she is no housewife, she is single.

Makyle: I was hoping you would say that.

Makayla heads back to I-20. Soon, they are at her nice condo in Decatur. Kay and her brother finally reach the condo. Makyle collects his luggage and follows his sister. Once inside, Ky stops and looks around.

Makyle: Nice!

Makayla: Thanks!

Makyle: This place needs to be featured in Better Homes and Gardens, Veranda or some magazine!!

Makayla: *(smiling)* You think? *(While holding up the latest issue of Atlanta Homes)*

Makyle flips through the open pages featuring his sisters beautifully decorated condo.

Makyle: Now these people really know talent. I'm proud of you sis.

Makayla: Thanks.

Makyle pulls a wrapped gift from his duffle and hands it to his sister.

Makyle: I'm really proud of you.

Makayla opens her gift to find a beautiful emerald green vase. Her eyes widen.

Makayla: This is so beautiful. More than beautiful, it is breathtaking---authentic?

Makyle: I suppose so. It came from that abandoned house I told you about.

Makayla: Oh, this is the piece you want me to check out?

Makyle: No, that's not it. But I do want you to have this piece.

Makayla: And I have just the right spot for it. (*She places it on an antique vanity sitting in her foyer*) Just look at it! It is gorgeous (*she hugs her brother*) Thanks a million!

Makyle: Just for you and I think it fits in quite well

Makayla: Perfectly!

Makayla picks up Ky's smaller bag and escorts him to the spare bedroom.

Makayla: Make yourself at home...unwind!

Makyle: (*Looking around at the beautifully decorated room in tones of pewter, chocolate, silver, and powder blue*) You make it very easy!

Makyle joins Makayla back in the great room where she is comfortable on the sofa munching on chips and dip and watching the Body Guard. The two reminisce and laugh and sip on wine. Eventually, Kay finds her brother has fallen asleep. She covers him and disappears into the bedroom.

The next morning Makyle awakens to the sound of light Jazz and the smell of bread and coffee. He makes his way into the kitchen.

Makayla: You whimped out on me.

Makyle: Yes, and slept like a baby. Love the scented candles. Thanks!

Makayla: All in the name of love

Makyle notices the table is set for four.

Makyle: Company?

Makayla: Oh yea, On Wednesday's Jaden and Justin come over for breakfast. They should be here any second.

Makyle: Good thing I got dressed.

Makayla: Yea, a good thing. *(Door bell rings-Ky opens the door.)*

Makyle: Hi, come in. *(Justin rushes past Ky to greet his Aunt Kay.)*

Jaden: Hi I'm Jaden, please forgive my son. He has this thing about Aunt Kay.

Makyle: Hello, I'm Ky---Come, Come, Come in! *(The two meet Kayla and Justin in the kitchen.)*

Jaden: Justin, that was rude.

Justin: I'm sorry.

Makyle: *(extends a hand)* I'm Kyle.

Justin: Justin. *(the two shake hands)* Are you and Aunt Kay really twins?

Makyle: According to our parents we are.

Justin: So, who is the oldest?

In unison, Ky and Kay say, "I am!" They laugh while being ushered to their seats by Kayla. They all enjoy their wonderful meal and exchange good conversation. All done, Kayla walks her friend outside.

Makyle: You have a great day!

Jaden: It certainly has gotten off to a great start. *(Outside in the car)* Sister, he is just gorgeous. (*She pulls off; Kayla goes back inside to find Kyle clearing the table.*)

Makayla: Gorgeous! And he does the dishes. (*Kyle glances at his sister*)

Makyle: Great meal, great company, every Wednesday huh?

Makayla: And sometimes twice on Sunday! (*They both laugh finishing up the dishes.*)

Makyle: Ready for walk or run?

Makayla: Sure. (*Sounding curious*)

Makyle: I'm going with you.

Makayla: Love it!

Makyle: I'm no marathon man, but I do like to keep in shape.

Makayla: Let's do it! (*The two head out for a nice walk. When they return Fed Ex is just pulling up.*)

Makayla: I wonder what that is. I am not expecting a package.

Makyle: Hope it is what I think it is. (*They both approach the delivery van. Kayla shows her ID. Ky receives the large package and takes it inside where he opens it.*)

Makyle: Now, this is what I have been telling you about. This piece of artwork. Do you think it is worth anything?

Makayla: (*In fascination*) Wow!

Makayla: It certainly appears aged and in fairly good shape. (*Looking at the signature at the bottom of the work.*)

Makayla: "Corot". So I have got to do some research. (*She stares at the piece for a few moments*).

Makayla: That beautiful vase, this awesome piece of artwork. My brother takes a plane. Ok, Ok- You have got my attention. I'm headed for the shower. I have a date with internet explorer-I've got some surfing to do.

Makyle: That's my sister! You've got that look. (*Kay heads towards her bedroom, pauses, then turns around*)

Makayla: What did you say?

Surprised to see that her brother was nowhere to be seen, she goes on for her shower. Afterwards, she sits down at her desk and googles. She learns of a French artist from the 1800's that painted bold colors—quite the opposite...this is apparently a lead and hand sketched drawing. Kayla goes into the Great Room, gets out her French interpretation manual and discovers that the piece is called "Lady at Dawn". It is an illustration. Kay realizes at this point she is probably going to need expert help in authenticating this piece. She gets out the yellow pages and searches for art authentication. She finds a few local names and underlines them. Again, she turns around and asks of Kyle...

Makayla: Ky, what's that? (*Just as before she finds no one*)

Makayla: (*thinking out loud*) Now I know it is time for bed. (*She logs out and heads towards her bedroom. The portrait is leaning on the wall outside her bedroom. She picks it up and looks it over once more.*

Makayla: So, I found a couple of guys that authenticate art.

Makyle: Oh yeah! So when do we check it out?

Makayla: Today! I'm just too excited. I have appointments at 1pm and 3pm. Both are in Alpharetta.

Makyle: Alpharetta..OK..Cool

Makayla slaps her brother on the shoulder with the newspaper and chuckles

Makayla: It's not too far out. (*She finishes in the kitchen and makes a few phone calls.*)

Kay goes to her closet and carefully picks out an outfit to wear. She looks just outside the door after hearing a light sounding noise to find that the portrait has fallen over.

Makyle: Ready to make the journey?

Makayla: It won't be that bad, come on.

They head up I-285 and 85 then finally Georgia 400. They find themselves at the address of a quaint French cottage style home. And are greeted by a seemingly nice gentlemen. A few moments later they arrive back at the jeep.

Makayla: What was that all about?

Makyle: You tell me, this your neck of the woods.

A few streets away the pair arrive at the home of John Poindexter as indicated on the mailbox. A gentlemen is standing in the front doorway. In a British accent John Poindexter says, "No, don't come to the front door, I'll meet you at the (as he points out) side door. As they follow instructions, KY protects the art piece from the out of control sprinkler. As they reach the side door they are greeted by a cute but barking Lassa Opso.

Poindexter: Come on in. Let's see? What have you got here?

Makyle unwraps the piece.

Poindexter: *(Quickly scanning the piece)* It is definitely old. *(Hesitating)* It's definitely a Corot, Uh, but in this condition a true collector of art would not take this serious! *(While staring at the piece and rubbing his British chin utters)* However, I can hold onto it and try to see what I can find out for you.

Makyle: (*carefully rewrapping the piece*) No, that won't be necessary. But thank you for your time. (*KY escorts his sister through the side door to their vehicle*).

Makyle: Just didn't like his attitude.

Makayla: He said he would hold onto it.

Makyle: I didn't trust him.

Makayla: (*Shaking her head*) OK!!

Makayla: Don't give me that Whoopee Goldberg Mississippi Burning look.

Makyle: Hey, you said it, not me. (*They speed off. The two find themselves in the peak of traffic on spaghetti junction*). *Give me a dirt road leading to a creek side anytime.*

Makayla: What? Kidding right?

Makayla: A lady at Dawn. That's an interesting title. Don't you think? Corot-I'd like to know more about him or her.

Makyle: (*Flashes that award winning smile*) Kay, you never cease to amaze me. He leans back and turns up the volume on V103 catching the Isleys' Harvest for the world.

The two find themselves back home safely after about 1.5 hours of playing in traffic. The two are eating a late dinner. KY reminds Kay that he will be leaving in a couple of days. Kay reinforces the fact that she will be leaving for New York in a few days as well).

A FEW DAYS LATER

Makayla is sitting on a Marta train, patiently waiting for her stop. The doors of the train open. To Kay's amazement, there is a woman who abruptly and rapidly rushes towards the open door then stops and stares. Her eyes penetrates Kays. "How weird", Kay thinks. This lady must be stuck in a time warp. She sporting a very fancy hair up do. The dress she's wearing reminds her of some "Aunt Jemima" attire. But Kay thinks, "OK, this is Atlanta, Five Points, midday on a Friday". As the train door closes, the woman is still standing there. Staring. The couple's eyes lock. Kay thinks, "Lady what is up with you? What do you want from me? What do you want from me, man!" I have to stop tripping. Kay makes her connection, gets into her Jeep and heads for home. No sooner than she steps inside her condo, she rushes towards the piece of artwork and tries to make some sense of what is going on. "Does this have anything to do with the woman at Five Points?" or "Am I just tripping?"

On the cell phone

Makayla: Makyle, It's me. You gotta tell me more about this abandoned house. I need to see it. In fact I'll be there this weekend. I have a score to settle with a ghost.

Kyle: Twin? You know I never question you. But what in the world?

Makayla: Baby brother just trust me on this one. Something is going on that even I cannot explain.

Justin: *(The boy is at the end of his favorite movie. He is in his jams as his mom comes into his room. While tucking him in and assuring him how much mommy loves him...Jaden boldly but honestly says)* "Mom, I don't like that lady at Aunt Kay's house".

Jaden: Lady? What Lady?

Justin: When I am at Aunt Kay's she just stands over my bed all the time. Not a word. Just stands looking at me.

A couple of days later Ky picks up his sister at the airport. They head down the highway and finally end up at a beautiful old antebellum style house. They go inside; antiques are everywhere.

Makayla: KY? When did you get into antiques?

Makyle: I told you! This old house had all this. This is where I got the vase and the art piece I brought to Atlanta.

Makayla: Ok, tomorrow I'm in

LATER THAT EVENING

Freddie B. pulls up and steps out of the most beautiful antique shiny black Chevrolet.

Makayla: Gorgeous, Gorgeous, Gorgeous!!

Freddie B: I try

The two embrace and lock eyes and lips, a soft one.

Freddie B: Lady, you still take my breath away.

Makayla: And you! Well!

Makyle: Ok you two, save some. B come on in and enjoy some of my famous catfish and puppies *(Arf, Arf)* beer galore!

Makayla: So Freddie, That Let'-Chevy. That is! Where did you get it?

Freddie B: I got it from one of the Bishops. He told me it washed up on the Tallahatchie. I fixed it up, brought it back to life. You like?

Makayla: Like it? Man! I've never!!

Freddie B: Well, later maybe we can go for a ride. *After the feast and several hours of childhood story swapping, Freddie B pulls off in his Let'*

Makyle: *(Instructs Kay to put on the gear)* You'll get it as soon as we head off the road. Besides, you don't want ticks to get on you.

Makayla: Ticks?

Makyle: Just put on the stuff! (*The two walk about ¼ of a mile then head off the main road. There's an obvious gravel road/path almost completely covered with grass, but obviously a road.*)

Makayla: How did you end up in this jungle?

Makyle: Hunting! (*After about a 15 minute walk through the thicket bottom*)

Makyle: Here she sits.

Makayla: (*Staring down at a run-down shack of a house*) You mean you went in there and survived? I'm surprised the darn thing didn't fall in on your rear end!

Makyle: Keep that in mind ok. (*Pushing back branches, approaching the shack; no broken windows, doors closed, KY opens the door and a squirrel runs out*)

Makayla: Oh crap! (*The two laugh*)

Makayla: You first

Makyle: (*Steps on the first board that partially falls in*) Be careful, Twin. If something happens we don't know who to sue.

Makayla: Oh, sure I do! You brought me in here.

They walk inside. Makayla seems to be in shock. She stares and begins to walk although in a daze. Everything is now in slow motion. Makayla investigates every inch of the four room house. Off to the left an old but simple piano. Hymn books are in place. She opens a letter mostly eaten by mice which is not legible. She walks around the kitchen. The stove, cabinet, dishes, and pans are all in place. Dust is everywhere. She opens the cabinet door to what she recognizes to be a pie cabinet. There are very old but nice dishes. Kay continues her travels off to a "side room". There she finds several trunks.

She opens the first one full of beautiful crystal, amber, crimson, and emerald china. Wow! Costume jewelry, beads, bracelets, ear bobs, broaches, and perfume bottles. Another trunk has shoes, belts, and hats. In the last trunk there are photographs, all in black and white. Sophisticates!! Ladies, gents, children, groups, beautiful couples, houses, flower gardens, fruit orchards, and parks! All the makings of a perfect family.

Kayla full circles to the big room, which from the looks of it served as a master bedroom, dining room, and sitting area. There is a fully made up bed, a tea set to the left, a dining table for six to the right. Straight to the front near the window is another beautiful old organ with a chair and sofa next to it. In the organ seat, Kayla finds a composition book listing names, dates, and times along with what could be a planner/date book. Inside are insurance policies for Tennessee Life, Georgia Compensation, and Atlanta survivor's benefits.

Get this......time of birth policy $3.00-worth at time of death if 60 years or older-$175.00.

Makayla: Ain't that something!? No wonder it is from different states. Black folks probably couldn't get insurance in the Sip in those days.

At the very bottom, the perfect find. "Oh my", Kayla repeats, "a beautiful portrait of a Negro woman". (Staring)

Kyle: Boo!

Kay: Darn it Kyle!

Kay notices the clothes line stretched from corner to corner in the great room. Hung carefully and on the far wall. Neatly there are dresses, skirts, shawls, and coats. Kay reaches out to the apparent linen dress. It is dry, thin, and old. It crumbles like crackers. Kay touches another, it crumbles. She remembers her camera, takes it out and begins taking shots of the line...click, click, click.

Ky: So are you back on earth?

Kay: I don't want to come back to earth. I don't want to come back to earth ever again. Is this unreal?

Ky: You're asking me?

Kay: See the newspaper? 1920! But that's the date of the paper. We don't know when someone last lived here. *As they leave the shack, Kay takes pictures of the old house...click, click, click. As they walk out, Kay notices on the side of the house a humongous rose bush so large-about the size of the a maple or magnolia tree.*

Kay: Ky, have you ever seen anything like this in your life?

Ky: How beautiful! How strange.

Kay: Strange?

Ky: I've never seen it before...all the time I've been hunting out here I should have seen something like that!!

Kay and Ky are both amazed. Kay pulls out her camera...click, click, click. The twins return to their safe haven.

Ky: Sis, you can shower first.

Kay: Thanks! (*Still half dazed, Kay hits the shower and returns fully dressed to the T - heels, beaded dress, hair up, the works*).

Ky: Off to the Grammies?

Kay: You just let me handle this...o.k!

Ky: Hey never mind me; handle your business girl. (*Saved by the knock.*)

Kay: I'll get it

In walks Freddie, so handsome! Not to speak dressed in white linen head to toe with a dozen roses for his lady. Kay invites Freddie inside and gives a light peck on the cheek as she accepts her beautiful bouquet.

Ky: Hello brother! (*The two exchange handshakes as Kay put her roses in water, an antique vase.*)

Kay: Twin! We'd like to chat but the Grammies await us. (*The two laugh lovingly.*)

The handsome couple exits. Once inside the Chevy, as though he could wait no longer—Freddie leans over and kisses his beautiful date. Just then the glove compartment falls open.

Freddie: That's weird. All this time this thing has been jammed (*Makayla notices an old broach.*)

Kay: (*picks it up*) What do we have here? Finders-keeper. (*She opens the heart shaped locket to find the photos of 2 beautiful babies. An inscription-"Thank you*

God for my blessed babies".) What beautiful children; their mother must have been proud.

Freddie: And look what good condition it's in.

The two find themselves after a very short drive facing the most romantic cabin. A rocky spring just off to the side. Kay can't believe her eyes.

Kay: Look at this place! Did you do this? (*Roses, wisteria, hanging moss everywhere*)

Freddie: Yes, you know I have always loved gardening.

Kay: My it's breath taking. The sound of the spring water seemed amplified. I don't remember it being this loud when we were kids-beautiful!

Freddie escorts his date inside to a table fit for a queen. It was all antique china no doubt. Beautiful flatware, candles, another breath taking moment for Makayla. The two enjoy a romantic meal, soft music and dancing.

In the background plays "Ain't it Fun Reminiscing". The two walk outside, the romance continues while sitting on a bench swing for two listening to the sound of spring water running over the rocks, the two are arm in arm.

Freddie: You know I love this place. When I'm here, I feel like nothing else matters.

Kay: I can certainly understand why.

Freddie: It's hard to believe that just a few miles from this place, nature is being slowly destroyed. What they're doing to the environment is just unbelievable.

Kay: So the Bishops haven't let up on the sale of timber?

Freddie: Not in the least-but enough about that. I have my heaven right here. And my own live angel-you know

Kay: Sometimes I feel so lost. But being here right now with you, nothing else really matters.

Kay: (*No words spoken-Just joy in her eye. Reminiscing the past, enjoying champagne and laughter.*)   It's good.

Background-Smokey Robinson-"Turn the lights down low-The two begin to slow drag, baby come close-(caressing) Put your hand in mine

Freddie: Oh, please be kind.

Freddie leads Kay to an elevation in the middle of the spring. Kissing-Let the fire start, so warm-you know

the rest. So warm. Fire flies galore appear-Just to celebrate their loving.

Freddie: Ok, this is for me. Imagine, outside in the woods-naked in the middle of a natural spring. The sound of the warm water running over the rocks, champagne flowing through your blood stream, surround by lights of fire flies. The crooning of Smokey Robinson in your ear. The heaviness of Freddie B. Oh, it doesn't get any better than this yall!! UH, UH.

Next morning, Freddie B and Kay kiss their good bye as he drops her off at the airport. Kay arrives at her apartment and begins to reminisce over what a good time she had with Freddie and turns the lights down low. Kay starts looking through some of her finds from the old house. The photographs, the composition book, the large portrait of this beautiful woman.

Kay: I know you! I've see you! Who are you? (*Kay goes to the old piece of art that Ky brought on his previous visit.*) Maybe this is the same woman in the art. (*Comparing the two*) No, as different as night and day.

Kay: She's white (*Kay pops in and out of the shower, packs a few things, calls her mom.*)

Kay: Mom! I don't believe you're all into my business like that.

Kay: I know that son of yours never could keep his mouth shut.

Kay: Love you mom, gotta go (as she answers the doorbell) Jaden's here, were going shopping

Jaden: Hi mom!

Kay grabs her purse as the two leave for some shopping good time. Makyle and Freddie pull up in the sheriff's car. The two get out at the corner store, pick up some supplies, and then walk to the bait shop. All eyes are on the two. The Bishops and no doubt, Roscoe.

Freddie: Yea! You see the Bishops, you see Roscoe.

Bishop: You two looking mighty carefree.

Roscoe: Bass biting?

Bishop: Yea, you never know what you gonna find when you go fishing.

Freddie: Roscoe, maybe you can go fishing with us sometime.

Roscoe: No! No! I don't go near haunted places.

Bishop: B, you got that Chevy looking mighty fine...fine lady, fine truck.

Roscoe: Just like a fish, that Chevy found a way to the top.

Ky: What's that Roscoe?

Roscoe: Yea, you got one fish and two frying pans. What you gonna put in the second frying pan?

Roscoe: You put plenty of grease. (*Only Roscoe is laughing at his joke.*)

Makyle and Freddie pull off. The Bishop and Roscoe watch them until they are out of sight.

Freddie: Roscoe was in rare form.

Ky: I suppose being a Lassie for the Bishops can make you that way. You can't blame everything on one bump on the head.

It is almost dark. Freddie and Ky decide to run by the old house. To their amazement, the windows were boarded up and "No Trespassing" signs were posted on the front door and a couple of trees.

Ky: What the...?

Freddie: Ain't this something!

Makyle: Yea! Somebody's been fishing!

Freddie: But they ain't been deep sea fishing!
Freddie gets out of his car and walks up to the front door which is all boarded up! He walks around to the back door...boarded up! As he's coming around the side of the house, he almost trips over a rock. He picks up the rock, "Allsin" is etched in the rock. He shows it to Makyle.

Makyle: Allsin? All sin? Who knows, this is quite a turn of events-no trespassing.

Freddie: Yea! Someone doesn't want us here! But why? (*Back in the house*)

Makyle: (*Begins looking through some of the collectibles he retrieved from the old house. He stares at some of the costume jewelry in particular.*)

Makyle: I wonder what she was like, the woman that would wear this. (*He leans back in his recliner as though to meditate. "Stormy Weather" is playing on the radio as he imagines the beautiful face of Lena Horn.*)

Makyle: Wow, I haven't heard that in a long time. (*Makyle notices the details in the jewelry. Hand-*

crafted no doubt. He notices on the clasp AP. Makyle holds the necklace in his hand and dozes off)

Makayla arrives at her condo and goes straight to her bedroom.

Makayla: I've got to finish packing. *(She notices the portrait.)* Do I leave you here?

Makayla: Maybe I should take you with me. I'll have something to focus on. <u>You can help me antique shop.</u> *(She chuckles. Suddenly a weird feeling comes over her. She feels as though the woman in the portrait agrees with her.)*

Makayla: What do you want from me?

The next morning Makayla parks her vehicle at the Avondale Kiss and Ride and hops on Marta. Just as the door closes, she gets a glimpse of a woman again staring at her, this time with her hand out-stretched. Makayla does not, cannot react. The next thing she hears is Hartsfield Jackson-your next stop is Hartsfield Jackson. This is the end of the line.

CHICAGO

A few hours later, Makayla is in her hotel room in Chicago. She tips the Bell Hop, closes the door and notices what a beautiful room. Makayla opens her suitcase and starts to unpack. She picks up the portrait of what has become a beautiful unknown friend.

Makayla: Who are you? Where did you go? Why did you leave all your beautiful things behind? I'm sure there was a man involved. Perhaps he took you away to a much more exquisite and exciting life than you could have in Abberton. I guess you didn't need any of that stuff. (*Makayla turns on the radio. First things she hears is "Stormy Weather".*) The oldies, not tonight, Next! Oh Maxwell!! Fortunate to have you girl. (*She walks over to the suitcase stares at the portrait. This time she notices the photo is two ply. Attached to what appears to be cardboard, to her surprised it is the front album cover of Lena Horn's "Stormy Weather".*)

Makayla: Oh my! Ok, I'm not going to freak out again Missy (*while staring at the portrait*) What do you want from me?

She stands the portrait upright on the chest of drawers "You're only a photograph. I've got the power in this room." Continuing to unpack, Makayla puts a few things in the drawers, picks up her beaded black dress, holds it up against herself as though it's a dancing partner.) Can't get you wrinkled.

Makayla: I'm gonna be looking fine sporting this tomorrow night! Yes! (*She hangs the dress and a couple of other things in the closet.*)

Makayla: This can wait—I'm tired. (*Without undressing, Kay flops onto the bed and falls asleep. Hours later, Makayla awakens to the calling of her name.*)

MAKAYLA

Makayla: What time is it? Oh my, after midnight! (*She stumbles into the bathroom. On return, she notices the photograph.*) You haven't fallen asleep yet?

Everything now in slow motion, as though in a trans she notices her makeup bag still packed, her suitcase still packed, cell phone and lap top neatly on the dresser, closet door open, party dress neatly hanging, bed all made up. Makayla walks over to her mysterious friend.

Makayla: So! You weren't going anywhere, you had just arrived, started unpacking and what? Where did you go? What happened?

Makayla picks up her cell. Her mom is on the other end, who fumbles as she finds her glasses and sticks in her false teeth after retrieving them from a glass filled with denture cleanser. She grabs her wig from the bed post and pops it on her head while grabbing her pistol from the bed stand.

Mom: Hello-girl don't be calling me while I'm busy

Makayla: Mom, mom, sorry mom. I meant to dialup Ky. Go back to sleep.

Mom: Sleep, who's asleep? I'm busy! (*They both hang up as Makayla shakes her head.*)

Ky: (*Reaches for the phone*) Hello!

Mom: She just woke me up!

Ky: It's ok. Mom, Kay's on the other line. Goodbye. Go back to sleep.

Mom: What are you talking 'bout? I got my own business. (*Mom drops dentures in the soak...glasses and wig still in tow*)

Makayla: I'm sorry if I woke you.

Ky: It's ok, what's up?

Makayla: We've been looking at this whole thing backwards.

Ky: Backwards? What whole thing? Slow down.

Makayla: We've been assuming that someone packed all their things, perhaps family who lived far away was supposed to come for the stuff and never did. I don't know.

Kay: Honestly? Did any of that stuff look like it belonged to some old person? No, it did not. Theory- what if this young woman arrived, began to unpack and something happened to her?

Ky: Like what? Did she just vanish? I'm sure no one around Abberton would admit knowing any such person.

Kay: It would seem so. But I'm not buying it. I'll be back down there in 2 days. I have a lot of questions to ask the good ole folks of Abberton. I also have some investigating to do in that old house.

Ky: Well, it won't be as easy to investigate as before.

Kay: What do you mean?

Ky: The house is boarded up and there are no trespassing signs everywhere.

Kay: What?

The next day, Kay meets with her client. They discuss the art décor, color, their lines, etc. Kay goes back the beautiful hotel room.

Kay: No trespassing, everything boarded up.

Kay: Unbelievable! *(looking up at her friend)* I certainly am glad I got you out of there. It must have been lonely there all this time!

Kay dresses for her evening out. As she put on her gown, she remembers the crumbling of the old clothing hanging on the make shift line in the quaint living room.

Kay: Lady! I bet you had some kind of class! *(Staring at her friend)* Why does it seem as though your heart is broken?

Later that night-Nice Ball Room. Gorgeous men wall to wall, the women, not bad either. Kay shares with her friend Melinda.)

Melinda: I'm so glad you called me when you got to Chicago.

Kay: Of course, you're my girl.

The two make their way through the dancing crowd, drinks in hand. They're both bobbing their head on the side lines when two hunks pull them both out on the dance floor. The girls are having a ball. They're out on the floor for what seems forever. As they make it back to their table, they're served with champagne.

Melinda: You know I had almost forgotten how much I love to party.

Kay: You couldn't swear that by me. (*The girls are chatting when they both notice this Goddess of a man approaching their table.*)

Kay/Melinda: (*In unison*) HIM!

Kay: Girl, his eyes are dead on you! I'm going to make myself disappear. I ain't mad at cha!

Kay makes her way through the ever so live crowd to the powder room. While freshening up, the most stunning woman comes into the powder room. Kay looking into the mirror-The lady in red with an accent-Kay cannot quite make out ....says all of this makeup and perfume)

Lady in Red: Do you think anyone uses it?

Kay: Probably not? (*Kay still looking into the mirror*)

Kay: What a beautiful evening gown! I know you probably hear this all the time but, has anyone ever told you...you look like...

Kay/Lady in Red: *(in unison)* "The legendary Ms. Horn"

The beautiful lady in red offers up this incredible smile which becomes chilling laughter. She throws her head back and lets out this powerful laugh, laughter that is as powerful as she is beautiful. Kay turns to meet the face of this beauty

Kay: What? *(There is no face, no lady. Kay turns back to the mirror. The lady in red is still laughing. Kay turns again-no one! She doesn't bother to look back into the mirror-Just leaves. All the while Kay is walking out of the powder room, she can hear and feel the power of this woman's laughter piercing at her back. Kay reaches her table as Melinda and "HIM" seem to be getting along quite well, however he is obviously making an exit)*

Him: You will be hearing from me.

Melinda: *(waves him off)* Bye Bye *(with a smile)*

Melinda: Is it supposed to be part of the appeal to be "from out of town?"

Melinda: Kay! Kay! Goodness you look like you've just seen a ghost!

Kay: Literally *(in the powder room)* someone just had an out of body experience. I don't know if it was me or the Lady in Red!

Kay: I need a drink. *(The waiter arrives just in time, Kay downs a ripple.)*

BACK IN ABBERTON

Kay stops at the corner store greeted by Bishop and Roscoe.

Bishop: Hey pretty lady. *(Kay nods cordially)*

Roscoe: I know a "pretty lady" just like you! Right here *(Roscoe taps at his left shirt pocket)* Wanna see? Right here.

Bishop: Don't mind Roscoe, no one has ever seen pictures of this supposedly "pretty lady" that he keeps in his wallet. *(Kay nods cordially)*

Bishop: You know there's been a lot of activity at the "old place" since you've been coming around.

Kay: "Old Place?" My coming around?

Bishop: Yea! You've been coming up from Atlanta.

Kay: So, you know my brother Makyle.

Bishop: Sure do. He's good people. Freddie too! It's my business to keep in the know around here. Just want to keep the peace.

Kay: Oh! So you're a peace officer?

Bishop: Huh, Huh...

Just at that time Freddie B's patrol car pulls up, he and Ky together, and motions to Kay. Kay walks over and gets in the back seat. They pull off. Shortly after they arrive at the old place.

Kay: Incredible! No trespassing! (No trespassing signs everywhere)

Kay: That's a switch; no guessing someone doesn't want us to be here.

Freddie B: You think?

Just as the trio are trying to take all this in, up pulls Bishop and of course Roscoe and a couple of other "gentlemen" in a separate vehicle. "Things look nasty".

Freddie: Sirs? *(As the group get out of their vehicles.)*

Bishop: Just thought you good folk might need assistance here.

Freddie: No, we're fine, just surprised to see all these "No trespassing" signs everywhere!!

Bishop: Oh! Don't bother bout that, just looking out for the concern and interest of the Good Folk" of Abberton.

Kay: Concern? And what concern might that be?

Bishop: You might be somebody in Atlanta but in these parts you're just another pica ninny.

All together-Ky, Freddie B, and Roscoe gesture to protect Kay, Bishop's men gesture as well, putting in full view their special weapons.

Roscoe: I won't let you hurt this lady-not another lady.

Freddie: It's Ok Roscoe, no one is going to be hurting anyone *(All weapons pointed at Freddie.)*

Roscoe: Not the Baby!! Not the baby!! *(Roscoe picks up the large Rock engraved on it ALLSIN. Gunshots are fired.*

****

The day is very hot. No rain for weeks. The dust is thick as the wagon pulls up, driven by a mean looking white man. He gets out of the wagon and reaches out his hand to help this distinguished looking woman "white-of course". They get out of the wagon. Sitting quietly at the back of the wagon is a black young Nigra boy.
The two adults approach the quaint house. The white man takes his cane and raps on the door. No one answers. He raps again, this time even louder and in repetition.

The front door opens and standing in the doorway is a beautiful Negro woman.

Negro woman: How can I help you?

White woman: You know why we are here! Where is she?

The negro woman remains in the doorway. A small tan skinned green eyed little girl appears in the doorway, hiding in the dress tail of the black woman.

White woman: There she is, Oh my God! What a beautiful child! Come here to me.

Unafraid, the little girl walks around to the woman.

White woman: Just look at her - cold black hair like silk, green eyes, lightly tanned skinned. Why! She's Taylor made and (*inspecting the child, first looking at her hands*) cuticles light, ears light, she ain't gonna get no darker than this. No one would ever know she had a drop of Nigra blood in her. Thank God your granddaddy was a white man.

Negro woman: But this is my baby-she's mine!

White woman: Wyleen what kind of life can you give this child? Nigra won't accept her. White folk will take advantage of her. I mean, Wyleen, you don't even know if our father or which of the 2 of my brothers is her daddy.

Negro woman: But she is my baby!

White woman: Let's make this simple. The child is going with me! I am sorry for your troubles. I didn't wait four years to continue to long for a daughter. I have even put this child's life in jeopardy by allowing her to be deprived for this long. And who knows who might have taken advantage of her.

Negro woman: Well, you know something about that don't you? The only somebody might taken advantage of her is standing right next to you. (*She looks at the old white woman.*)

White woman: Now, look here. I've kept track of this child. Visiting every now and then. Wondering if her beautiful hair didn't nap up. Thank God, she was blessed with her father's blood! I can just imagine what a beautiful young lady she will grow up to be.

Negro woman: For to be a House Nigger???!!!

White woman: Don't you understand what I have been telling you? This is the daughter I have been waiting for Precious, your new life is waiting for you. (*As she leans down to stroke the child's beautiful hair.*)

Negro woman: No! (*Both fear and anger in her eyes*) No! Not my baby! (*The white man and the young black boy gesture to ensure the white woman's protection.*)

Negro woman: Deal! There ain't no deal!

White woman: Here are the papers, you just need to sign and we're all done.

Negro woman: What's going on here?

White woman: Now, don't be foolish or difficult. This is the deed to 100 acres of land including the house and the lake you're standing on. You don't even have to be uprooted.

Negro woman: Never! I will find another place to live. Just leave me and my baby be! *(White woman takes the deed and tries to force the woman to sign.)*

Negro woman: No! I tell you No! *(The little girl starts to cry as she sees her mommy so upset.)*

Child: Mommy! Mommy!

White woman: *(Throwing the deed on the ground she stomps over and slaps the Negro woman to the ground.)* See you're upsetting the child!

Child Rushes to her mommy and holds onto her belly as her mommy remains kneeling on the ground.
White woman, no doubt with a look of victory, walks over and picks up the child. The little girl is so graceful and unrebellious.

Child: Yes *(as she nods her head).*

Child: *(She looks down and whispers)* My mommy.

White Woman: *(looking into the eyes of the child)* It's mother.

The group walks towards the wagon. The white woman seems so proud to have a baby in her arms. They all board the wagon. The negro woman walks toward them. They begin to ride away (getty up/hah). The negro woman begins to walk faster and faster until she is running and crying out.

Negro woman: My baby, my baby!!

Child: Mommy! Mommy! (*She looks back and sees the agony of her mommy. She breaks away from the woman and goes to the back of the wagon-arms stretched out*) Mommy!!

The wagon slows, the negro woman is still approaching the wagon. The old man stands up with whip in hand and lashes out at the distressed woman.

The child, wailing out, jumps off the wagon into the arms of her mommy as though she knows this is the only way to protect her. They both fall to the ground arm in arm. The wagon continues moving as the group watches them kneeling on the ground. The Madonna and child are back together.

What a site to behold. A beautiful teenage girl and young man run across the field. They playfully disappear inside an abandoned barn. The two are quite charming and obviously quite fond of each other. They fall onto a large heap of hay. It seems this isn't the first time they've had such carrying on.

Roscoe: You know you look like a panther?

Carrie Jean: A panther?

Roscoe: Yea! Just now when you wuz running, you look like a panther.

Carrie Jean: And just where did you see this panther that you are putting my looks up against?

Roscoe: Never seen none, 'cept in a book.

Carrie Jean: I wish I really could run like a panther. I would run so far away from here.

Roscoe: Leave me here? I mean leave your mommy here?

Carrie Jean: You see, I just can't win. You see how colored folks looks at me, especially the women. I can't make just one friend. And the white, well they just want to use me. And I do want to do everything right! All my church going and everything. I pray so hard. God do you even hear me?

Carrie Jean: Is it a game we play every day of our lives trying to find what we believe is right? I've made so many mistakes, so many times with tears in my eyes trying to live with my regrets...searching for heaven. (*Alicia Keys, "Search for Heaven".*)

Roscoe: Carrie Jean you 'bout to die? You 'bout to go to heaven? Ain't you too young for heaven?

Carrie Jean: (*Takes a deep breath then sigh as she looks at her only friend.*) We live in a world where you're taught that beauty is skin. (*Looking at her own skin knowing "what she hears people saying 'bout her*) My high yellow skin, makes me dazed and confused. I feel like I'm losing. But there's a God up there and he tells me I'm going to win. So why do I feel crazy searching for heaven? Heaven ain't nowhere near this place.

Roscoe: Heaven ain't...isn't (*as he reminds Carrie Jean she's the proper one*).

Carrie Jean: (*Looking deeply into the eyes of her unassuming but true friend*) I wish you could for one moment understand me.

Roscoe: I understand it. Heaven is right here. Right in my heart (*Roscoe pats over his heart*). And Carrie Jean is my heart. So you will always be in heaven. So you stop that looking and stay right here by me.

The two cover themselves in the heap of hay. After they enjoy one another, they hear the sound of a pick-up truck and loud noises.

Carrie Jean: Roscoe (*as she stands and straightens up herself*).

Roscoe: It's old Bishop and somma his boys. They come out here to get drunk so the woman folk won't know they wrong doings.

Carrie Jean: And you brought me out here?! Darn it Roscoe!!

Roscoe: They usually don't come here-least I'm with them. White folks don't go 'round nigra parts least they have a nigra with them.

Carrie Jean: Well I guess they just found themselves two nigras huh?

Roscoe: I'm going out front. You slip out back and run as fast as you can "Like a panther" to you momma's house.

Just as Carrie Jean is about to exit the back way an ole' red neck meets her face to face.

Red Neck: Going somewhere my pretty?

Carrie Jean: (*with fear in her eyes-but remembering the words of her mommy, "Don't ever fear white folk, that's where they get their power-from the fear of nigras"*) I'm on my way home that's all.

Red Neck: But why so fast? Don't you want to wait for your boyfriend? (*Carrie Jean could hear the sound of Roscoe being slapped around*)

Carrie Jean: (*As she runs back inside to save her friend*) Why are you doing this? We haven't bothered anyone.

Bishop: (*Standing over Roscoe*) Well!! Well!! So how did you learn to talk like that? If I didn't know any better, I would think a proper white lady was standing in front of me. Looks like you mammy's been teaching you good, too bad she forgot to teach you how to respect white folk. (*He starts to tear at Carrie Jean's dress. Carrie Jean pushes him away. Bishop slaps Carrie Jean's beautiful face.*)

Bishop: I know you don't think you were put here on earth for the pleasure of a "Retard" like Roscoe, now do you?

Roscoe: Don't hurt Carrie Jean, my Carrie Jean.

Carrie Jean: Roscoe, it's ok if I have to.

Roscoe: No Carrie Jean, you don't have to.

Bishop: I guess we just might have to start back lynching in these part (*as he spits a large wad of tobacco juice near Roscoe's foot*) to remind nigras just where they belong.

Roscoe guards Carrie Jean with his slim body. Bishop leans towards Roscoe. As he does, he steps on a hay fork that is buried in the heap of hay. The hay fork stabs him in his chest as he yells out. His men focus on his needs. Roscoe and Carrie Jean, the two of them run like panthers. Later at Carrie Jean's mother's house, they stumble onto the porch.

Man: Wyleen, he's hurt (*As two of Bishops men carry him and lay him on Ms. Wyleen's porch*).

Man: Don't just look at him, he needs tending to. That gal of yours and her retard boyfriend did this.

Ms. Wyleen: Carrie Jean?

Man: Just tend to Mr. Bishop, we will take care of those two later.

Ms. Wyleen: (*Opens the door. Bishop is carried in by his men. As she tends to his wounds she prays.*) Mr. Bishop please have mercy on my baby Carrie Jean!

Later that evening, Ms. Wyleen opens the door to the back room. Carrie Jean is packing the few things she owns.

Ms. Wyleen: Carrie Jean!

Carrie Jean: Momma, I have to leave this place before I end up dead. By Bishop's hand or maybe by my own! I have to leave this place.

Ms. Wyleen: Where are you going?

Carrie Jean: Didn't you tell me you had kin in Chicago?

Ms. Wyleen: I don't know if they will welcome you or if they even know about you. We haven't kept in touch.

Carrie Jean: What? No momma, I'm leaving this place. I love you but I have to leave you and this place and my only friend Roscoe. Momma please take care of Roscoe for me.

Ms. Wyleen walks back to the front room where Bishop lays on the couch. She wakes him by poking him with a pair of scissors. Bishop stares at Ms. Wyleen with fear in his eyes. Ms. Wyleen cuts loose his bandage. Bishop starts to bleed through the bandage. With fear in his eyes, he says nothing.

Ms. Wyleen: (*As she pokes his wounds*) if anything bad happens to my Carrie Jean, look! This here nigger gon' kill you! DEAD!! (*Ms. Wyleen goes to the front door and opens it and yells out.*) Roscoe!!

Roscoe hurriedly comes into the house, gathers up Bishop, puts him in Ms. Wyleen's pickup and drives off. The next morning, Ms. Wyleen goes to the back room and opens the door. As she feared, no Carrie Jean. Ms. Wyleen takes a deep breath as she places her hand over her heart. Just about that time Roscoe pulls up in the pickup with his face beaten.

Ms. Wyleen: (*noticing his pain*) Where did you take her?

Roscoe: Nowhere. Don't know where she bout. Been over to the Depot, no Carrie Jean. (*The two head for the pickup. They reach the Depot. Still late dawn, the train is pulling off as they arrive.*)

Ms. Wyleen: (*Hurrying out of the truck, walking fast towards the train*) Carrie Jean!! Please baby! (*arms outstretched*) My baby, my baby!

Carrie Jean: Mommy, please forgive me. I love you mommy! I swear I love you! Please take care of Roscoe!

Roscoe sits in the pickup and bangs his head on the steering wheel! How awful and sad the sound of the horn beeeeep! Ms. Wyleen finally falls to the ground as she watches the beautiful face of Carrie Jean fade away.

꙳꙳

A few week later, Roscoe walks into the corner store trying to look "normal".

Store Keeper: Well Roscoe, you look like your best friend just died. (*Bishop and the store keeper begin to laugh*)

Roscoe: My friend ain't dead. But she's in heaven (*as he places his hand over his heart*).

Bishop: Now you don't think that gal loved you, do you? Why would she run off and leave you like that? You just need to get your mind off that gal!

Roscoe: Mr. Bishop you got any work for me?

Bishop: Now that's more like it. I supposing I do, plenty!!

Roscoe: For pay?

The next few weeks Roscoe did nothing but work, bailing hay, chopping cotton, picking cotton, pulling corn, feeding cows, slopping pigs, you name it).

Roscoe: *(As he walks up to the porch of the large two story antebellum home)* Mr. Bishop, I come for my pay. I wants my pay now. *(Bishop is relaxed in a brim hat, beige linen suit. He leans back in his rocker and props his legs up while enjoying a cigar and freshly made lemonade.)*

Bishop: Roscoe, now be reasonable. Ain't no law that says I have to pay a nigra for doing what he was born to do.

Roscoe: *(Boldly stepping onto the porch)* I wants my pay!

Bishop: *(sits straight in his rocker, pushes his hat back on his head)* Roscoe, you know I've taken care of you just about ever since your folks was killed in that accident.

Roscoe: I hear.....tell it wasn't no accident.

Bishop: I'd say you owe me a few more days work.

Roscoe: I come for my pay!

Bishop: I think you should best get off my property. (*Bishop notices the suitcase Roscoe is carrying. He reaches for the suitcase*) Going somewhere?

Roscoe: (*steps away from Bishop's reach*) Just want my pay!

Bishop: (*with confidence, sits back in the rocker*) I said off my property!

Roscoe: (*Mumbles under his breath*) I wonder what nigra or po' white family you swindled this property from?

Bishop: What? (*As he starts to rise but to his surprise is pushed back by Roscoe. Roscoe has taken out his blade and puts it to Bishop's throat.*)

Roscoe: I will be getting my pay.

Bishop tries to struggle with Roscoe but without success as he loses his balance and notices the blood shooting from his neck. He falls back into his rocker, holding pressure on his throat with his pocket handkerchief. Roscoe rushes into the house. He knows just where to go. He heads straight to the dining room, confident that no one is in the house as he is so familiar with the Bishops routine. He pulls open the top drawer of the nicely decorated side board. Roscoe knows what he is

The next few weeks Roscoe did nothing but work, bailing hay, chopping cotton, picking cotton, pulling corn, feeding cows, slopping pigs, you name it).

Roscoe: *(As he walks up to the porch of the large two story antebellum home)* Mr. Bishop, I come for my pay. I wants my pay now. *(Bishop is relaxed in a brim hat, beige linen suit. He leans back in his rocker and props his legs up while enjoying a cigar and freshly made lemonade.)*

Bishop: Roscoe, now be reasonable. Ain't no law that says I have to pay a nigra for doing what he was born to do.

Roscoe: *(Boldly stepping onto the porch)* I wants my pay!

Bishop: *(sits straight in his rocker, pushes his hat back on his head)* Roscoe, you know I've taken care of you just about ever since your folks was killed in that accident.

Roscoe: I hear.....tell it wasn't no accident.

Bishop: I'd say you owe me a few more days work.

Roscoe: I come for my pay!

Bishop: I think you should best get off my property. (*Bishop notices the suitcase Roscoe is carrying. He reaches for the suitcase*) Going somewhere?

Roscoe: (*steps away from Bishop's reach*) Just want my pay!

Bishop: (*with confidence, sits back in the rocker*) I said off my property!

Roscoe: (*Mumbles under his breath*) I wonder what nigra or po' white family you swindled this property from?

Bishop: What? (*As he starts to rise but to his surprise is pushed back by Roscoe. Roscoe has taken out his blade and puts it to Bishop's throat.*)

Roscoe: I will be getting my pay.

Bishop tries to struggle with Roscoe but without success as he loses his balance and notices the blood shooting from his neck. He falls back into his rocker, holding pressure on his throat with his pocket handkerchief. Roscoe rushes into the house. He knows just where to go. He heads straight to the dining room, confident that no one is in the house as he is so familiar with the Bishops routine. He pulls open the top drawer of the nicely decorated side board. Roscoe knows what he is looking for - "The easy get to stash". He takes several bundles of cash and some coins, then leaves the rest as he found it. As Roscoe rushes out of the dining room, he notices a large portrait of Bishop enjoying a large glass of tea. Roscoe pauses, then returns to the sideboard, opens the drawer, and takes the remaining cash. He looks into the wall mirror.

Roscoe: My pay! *(Roscoe hears the whistle of the noonday train. He rushes out of the house. He notices Bishop has managed to stand on his feet.)*

Bishop: Roscoe, I'm dying.

Roscoe: Bishop, you too mean to die. Least the devil himself done got sicka you!

Bishop: *(Falls back into his rocker while holding the <u>rag</u> in place around his neck, cries out)* UGH!!

Roscoe steps off Bishop's property and begins running toward the sound of the noonday train. He knows he has time because the train always slows down when it crosses over Main Street in town. Running through trees and puddles, Roscoe stops near the tracks and wait for the train. To his surprise, he can hear the sound of pick-up trucks and voices. He know this has to be Bishop's men. Roscoe starts to run toward the train. He cannot wait for the train to come to him. He has to meet it head on. Suitcase in fist, money bag tied tightly to his belt loop. Roscoe steps on the tracks and begin to run. The sound of the train is so powerful. It seems just as eager to meet Roscoe. Running, running, running, choo choo, choo choo, choo choo. The pace is so intense. Roscoe is now clutching the suitcase under his arm and running. The money bag falls. This is unknown to Roscoe. Roscoe sees the face of the train. Roscoe stops. He has to find a clearing to exit the tracks. He realizes his money bag is no longer at his side.

Roscoe: My pay! My pay!! (*Roscoe turns back, begins to run in the opposite direction knowing the train is behind him. He must find his pay. He sees the bag as he continues towards it.*)

Roscoe: (*in the most humble voice*) Thank you Master Jesus! (*He bends over to pick up the bag. Losing his bearing, Roscoe falls off the tracks into the sideline of trees. With the look of defeat on his face, Roscoe begins to sob. But suddenly, he sees the face of his beautiful Carrie Jean and stands to his feet. Stumbling at first, all belongings in tow, straightens his stance.*)

Roscoe: (*taking a sigh*) Like a panther. (*Roscoe runs and catches up to an open box car and throws himself onto the train.*)

※※※

With not even a glance towards Roscoe, the servant collects the dining ware from the passengers.

Servant: Enjoyed your meal? Anymore for you sir? I'll be back with lemonade.

The door opens to the car. In walks an attendant who walks right up to Roscoe. Attendant, says nothing, just stands. Roscoe opens his suitcase, removes an envelope and hands it to the attendant.

Attendant: *(Reading to himself)* "I do expect the safe arrival of my driver Roscoe P. Hutchenson in Overton, IL on July 1st. I also expect that I shall find him and all his belongings in proper order <u>including</u> this letter." He will be collected by my staff. Respectfully, The honorable Nathaniel Paul Bishop, Chancellor Township of Abberton, Ky."

The attendant hands the mail back to Roscoe. Roscoe opens an attractive box. The attendant takes two of the nice cigars along with a crisp American bill.

Attendant: Good ole Kentucky. (*He nods to Roscoe. Roscoe, having never looked up, receives the nod. As the attendant walks away, Roscoe places everything back into the suitcase. Then, he begins to eat a roll and* *sips water from a sterling silver flask with engravements that displays a beautiful heard of horses.)*

RESTAURANT IN CHICAGO

Carrie Jean's hair is well brushed. The length is tightly wrapped into a nice bun. She is not wearing any makeup. However, her skin is flawless. Her gray uniform is neatly pressed. Her apron is crisp and white.

Carrie Jean: May I take your order? (*She takes the order then walks to the next table.*)

Carrie Jean: What will you be having today sir? (*As Carrie Jean is about to take the two orders to the kitchen, she notices a stunning young white lady sitting alone. She walks over to her table.*)

Carrie Jean: (*Walks over to the lady*) May I offer you a menu? I'll be right back to take your order.

Lady: Tea! I'll have tea, cold, no sugar please, just lemon. Never sugar, always lemons.

Carrie Jean: Iced tea coming up. (*She walks away and notices the young lady's proper mannerism. As she* *thinks to herself, "What a fine young woman.")* I finally see the woman I've heard about so often. *(Returns with a tasty looking glass of tea.)*

Carrie Jean: Here you are, enjoy! Anything else ma'am?

Lady: *(No words spoken, just a nod of the head, then...)* More lemons please!
Later, Carrie Jean finds the café almost empty. However, the "proper lady" was still there. Carrie Jean walks back to her table.

Carrie Jean: So did you enjoy your tea? Would you like another?

Lady: No, I come here mostly for the scenery. *(She glances at the handsome man behind the counter.)*

Carrie Jean seems to be surprised to see this woman <u>admiring</u> a "dark skinned colored man".

Lady: I know you've noticed. It's ok to look at them. We won't be struck down by lightening. We just can't let our father's know. It's for their own good really. I mean that our fathers don't know.

Carrie Jean: *(Confused)* Yes, for their own good.

Later, Carrie finds herself back in her room. It's actually quite nice. She sits on her bed and begins to read letters.

Carrie Jean: My beloved mommy, I miss you dearly! *(She lays her head on her pillow and stuffs the letter under it.)*

NEXT DAY

Carrie Jean is serving up coffee. She notices her proper friend's arrival. She takes her same seat near the window in the sun. Completing her current order, Carrie Jean walks over to the lady.

Carrie Jean: Miss? *(No response from the lady)*

Carrie Jean: Mam, may I take your order please?

Lady: Tea! No sugar!

Carrie Jean: Would you like lemons?

Lady: No, never lemons!

Carrie Jean leaves and returns shortly with tea, sugar, and lots of lemons. Starring at Carrie Jean, the lady then cries out in laughter.

Lady: So what's your story?

Carrie Jean: My story?

Lady: Yea, we all have a story as to why we cross the tracks.

Carrie Jean: (*looking puzzled*) Well!

Lady: Yea, I come here for the scenery and the lemons. What about you? Are you getting back at your old man? Like most of us, we know that if we really want to stick it to our fathers, just take one look at a colored man. And for his own sake, just don't let the poor colored guy even know you're interested.

Carrie Jean: So, you are here to find a good looking colored man to marry up with?

Lady: Like that would ever happen. I just enjoy looking, and you?

Carrie Jean: The pay is good.

Lady: I'm not buying that. You can't hide behind that apron. (*Extending her hand*) I am Miss Abbigayle Applewhite, daughter of Jonathan and Margaret Applewhite.

Carrie Jean: (*Shaking the lady's hand*) I don't have any. My parents, I don't have parents.

Lady: What about a name? Do you have a name?

Carrie Jean: Allison...Allison Portwine.

Lady/Abbigayle: Greetings, Allison. Allison Portwine who doesn't have any parents. Oh! You don't have to spill your guts to me. A girls gotta do what a girls gotta do. What do you say? Let's blow this joint?

Carrie Jean: This is my job! I need this money!

Lady/Abbigayle: Just for today. If you hang with me, you won't need this job.

Carrie Jean: At least I owe it to the guys to let them know I'm leaving.

She takes off her apron and tells one of the other servers she's taking off for a break. She goes into the back to gather her belongings. Surprisingly, through open window she hears...

Roscoe: Psst! Carrie Jean! Psst! Carrie Jean, Hey Carrie Jean.

Carrie Jean: *(Not believing her ears, she looks out the window.)* Roscoe! Not now! Roscoe! *(Carrie Jean leans on the door in disbelief.)*

Roscoe: *(The face of relief and victory, knowing he has found his beloved, Roscoe climbs through the window).* Hi ya' doing Carrie Jean?

Carrie Jean: My friend is waiting for me!

Roscoe: That white lady ain't nona your friend. Roscoe is your friend.

Carrie Jean: *(Hugs her Roscoe)* Yes Roscoe, you are my friend. My only dear friend. Please don't mess this up for me.

Roscoe: Ain't you happy to see me?

Carrie Jean: Yes! Yes! I am *(she hugs Roscoe again)* She thinks I'm white!

Roscoe: Carrie Jean, I thought you sicka white!

Carrie Jean: Roscoe, please do this for me! I just want to be free to play just for a little while. I will come back for you tomorrow. Meet me outside tomorrow. Roscoe, how did you find me? How did you get here? Are you ok? My momma, how is she? Do you have a place to stay?

Roscoe: Just go! Go on! Play today. Roscoe a big boy, Roscoe's a man! (*Intelligently, he postures*) Tomorrow we discuss this.

Carrie Jean: Thank you! Thank you my friend. I love you Roscoe. *(She gives Roscoe another big hug and a kiss on the cheek)* I've got to go!

Roscoe climbs back out through the open window.

Roscoe: Carrie Jean loves Roscoe, yup! That's what she said.

Carrie Jean: *(looking in the mirror)* High yellow my foot!

Outside, Abbigayle is waiting for her new found friend. Carrie Jean/Allison gets in the car. Off they go! The two enjoy a day of getting their hair done, shopping, taking in a movie, wow!)

As they take off again in the car...

Allison: This is the life!

After a short drive to the country, Abbigayle pulls her car up to a beautiful home. The girls collect their shopping boxes. Allison follows along as Abbigayle rushes inside the beautiful paradise.

Abbigayle: Mother! Mother!

A tall distinguished woman approaches, a young colored man with her. She escorts him to the front door as she tells him…

Woman: I will no longer need your services. (*She dusts her hands as she exclaims*) What nerve stealing from me after I've been so good to him. Well! Darling, my dear Abby! (*She stares at the strange woman from head to toe.*)

Abby: Mother, this is my dear friend Allison! Allison, meet Ms. Jonathan Applewhite.

Allison: Nice to meet you Ms. Applewhite

Woman: You can call me Ms. Margaret. Abby, did you say dear friend?

Allison: Ms. Margaret. (*Allison extends her hand.*)

Woman: (*Looks again at Allison from head to toe, then says to her daughter...*) Abby, I shall meet you in the parlor.

Abby: (*Looking at her friend*) Have a seat, wait for me right here.

Woman: Abbigayle Applewhite!

Abby: No mother, it's not what you think.

Ms. Margaret: And just what do I think? Do I think you're just board out of your mind once more? Do I think you need another female to compete with other than your mother? Tell me Abbigayle, just what do I think?

Abby: She's a nice girl. Probably just wanting to get away from her parents for a while. You know...spread her wings, try living on her own. Or just plain bored herself. You'll see, she'll probably soon grow tired of us and go back to where she came from.

Ms. Margaret: And where is that exactly?

Abby: Well, she works at one of the Boutiques in town. She says she's completely on her own. No parents.

Ms. Margaret: Quite an independent young lady, it seems.

Abby: Yes, quite independent.
Abby turns to collect her friend. She sees Allison admiring the organ in the corner.

Abby: Can you play?

Allison: *(Knows she's only laid her hands on such a beauty for cleaning only. She many times played around and pretended to be an organist at the Bishop's when no one was watching.)* I do, I do, I do play.
Allison begins to play the organ as though she's been playing all her life. Allison thinks to herself, "God, what did you just do?" She sits there and play and sings in completion "Amazing Grace". Both Abby and Ms. Margaret just stare with tears in their eyes.

Allison: Thank you *(she thinks to herself)* God thank you!!

Ms. Margaret: I can finally stop paying for your lessons. *(As she looks at her daughter, then stares deeply into Allison's eyes).*

Ms. Margaret: I never would have guessed. (*The two women, Allison and Ms. Margaret, strangely enough stare at each other.*)

Ms. Margaret: Where did you study?

Allison: I...I...

Abby: Mother! It doesn't matter. She plays so beautifully. (*Abby takes her friend by the arm and escorts her to the guest bedroom.*)

Abby: You'll be staying here.

Allison: Here! Abby! But I couldn't! This is too much. You've done so much already.

Abby: Don't be silly, we have more than enough room.

Allison: But what about your mother's wishes?

Abby: It is my mother's daily wish and prayer to please me. All the while knowing that is impossible

Allison: I suppose you know your own mother.

Abby: I suppose I do! We'll get the rest of your things tomorrow (*As she leaves the room*).

Allison in disbelief, begins to remove her new wares from the boxes. She pressed one dress against herself and truly admires what she sees as she dances in front of the mirror.

The door opens, in walks Ms. Margaret.

Ms. Margaret: Well, Allison *(sipping a glass of tea and sits one glass on the serving tray)* Do you take lemons? I brought a few.

Allison: No! Never lemons but thank you for the tea. You are so kind.

Ms. Margaret: You know, lemons have many uses. While I do not take lemons with my tea, I use them on my skin.

Allison: Your skin?

Ms. Margaret: Yes, lemons are perfect for keeping the face white. See, look at me. I bet you'd never know I had a nose full of freckles. Wiping with lemons after cleaning keeps the face lily white. I'm sure you will find them quite useful.

Allison: As I said before, you're just too kind. Thank you for everything.

Abby: (*Entering Allison's room*) "Knock Knock" I hope you're ready to roll. To her pleasure, Allison was definitely ready to "roll", she looked stunning.

Allison: I'm ready to go but I don't know where to.

Abby: First thing, we are going to go and pick up your last paycheck. Secondly, we are going to find you a job at a nice boutique in town.

Allison: Boutique in town? (*Allison didn't resist*)

Abby: Yes! Mother believes those who are on the other side of the tracks should stay on the other side of the tracks. (*off they went*)

The ladies approached the shack of a restaurant.

Abby: I'll wait for you here.

Allison goes inside, shortly voices are heard, argumentative in fact, just as Abby starts to get out of the car.

Roscoe: Miss Ma'am! You wait right here that don't sound like no job for you to get into. (*Roscoe enters to find the head cook yelling at his Carrie Jean.*)

Cook: You didn't finish out the week. You get no check you hear. (*As he raises his hand to her*)

Roscoe: (*Grabs the cooks hand*) Oh don't think you liable to outa do that least you want that to be the last time you do anything! You best be getting the lady her pay.

Cook: Who are you?

Roscoe: (*As he picks up a black iron skillet from the stove*) The lady's pay!

Cook: (*Walks to the register*) Here! Now get out and don't ever come back!

Roscoe: (*Tips his hat*) That you can count on (*looks at Carrie Jean for agreement*)

Allison: Thank you Roscoe. (*They walk out*) My name is Allison. Allison <u>Portwine.</u> Please Roscoe, Allison ok! (*As they approach Abby waiting in the car*)

Abby: (*Looking at Roscoe while Allison climbs into the car*) Thank you.

Roscoe: Roscoe, I'm Roscoe.

Abby: Thank you Roscoe

Roscoe: (*Turning his attention to Allison*) I s'pose I can forget handy working around this place of business.

Abby: You were helping a friend. Losing your job for a friend. I think that's commendable. I'll just have to help you find another one. Can you drive?

Roscoe: (*Trying his hardest not to give himself away*) Yes, driving is one thing I do very good. Where to ladies?

Roscoe finds it to be quite a challenge driving in the city. But to both Allison's and Roscoe's advantage, Abby is too busy getting to know her new best buddies to notice. They go to store after store, traffic light after traffic light. The threesome seem quite comfortable as Roscoe chauffer's them around the city. Hours later they find themselves at Abby's instructions and direction, of course, at a beautiful lake front. The view of the city is at their disposal. Roscoe parks the car and spreads a picnic fit for Royalty. Roscoe takes this time to relax in the car. Legs propped, hat over his face as he tries to understand what is happening to himself and his beloved Carrie Jean.

Abby and Ally dance in the grass, laugh and talk about their dreams, enjoy some card playing and just enjoy the makings of a beautiful summer day and friendship.

Abby: Mother expects me to get married or at least be engaged by fall or it's off to college for me.

Allison: So, you have a beau? How exciting!

Abby: I wouldn't exactly say a beau, but there's this one gentleman that mother has her eyes on for me.

Allison: Do you at least find him appealing?

Abby: He's definitely the right kind of man.

Allison: So, you definitely don't love him?

Abby: I've never been in love so how am I supposed to know if I love him?

Allison: This gents got some work to do.

Abby: So, how about you? Are you running away from love?

Allison: No, actually I am searching for something. *(She looks at Roscoe knowing this is the one love she can and always will count on.)*

Abby: Searching? Oh.

Allison: Yes, I'm searching for heaven

Abby: Heaven!

Allison: Oh, that's just something I tell myself. The only place I'll find love, true love, is in heaven.

Abby: Well Ally, don't be surprised if some day you find a little bit of heaven right here on earth.

Allison: Ha! Ha! (*As she thinks to herself..."Right now I think I have died and gone to heaven." She takes a deep breath and admire the beauty that surrounds her.*)

Allison: Yes, just maybe heaven has found me.
(*A few hours later the threesome arrive at the Applewhite estate. Roscoe hesitant as this brings to mind Bishop Plantation.*)

Roscoe: (*Whispers to Allison*) You sure you want to stay here?

Allison: Yes! Roscoe, I promise you they are good people.

Roscoe: Good people? White people good people? (*Greeted at the door*)

Ms. Margaret: Youth! What a beautiful thing to have- just living life, no responsibility.

Abby: (*kiss, kiss on each of her mother's cheeks*) This is Roscoe.

Roscoe: (*Puts down a bag and wipes his hands on his pockets then extends for a hand shake*) Lovely to meet you ma'am.

Abby: I think he makes a fine driver and I'm sure you could find him quite useful around the estate.

Ms. Margaret: Oh!?

Roscoe: Yes ma'am, for pay!

Ms. Margaret: A place to sleep, 3 squares, and clothing. I'd say that's quite a handsome pay!

Roscoe: All that and a little pay sounds right handsome. Yea, right handsome.

Ms. Margaret: (*Before she could say another word the cutest little dog runs up to Roscoe's feet and starts to sniff. Roscoe bends over to pet the little one. "Look like belle has given the go ahead". Abby show Roscoe to his quarters.*) I'll talk to him later.

Abby: Mother! A <u>dog</u>! When did you get her/him?

Ms. Margaret: Her! Today.

Abby: I love her.

Roscoe: (*Still petting the dog*) I have to say this one thing, I never been kissed in the face by a dog before. No never been kissed by a dog and I don't think we might outta keep doing so. (*Roscoe stands and all the ladies begin to laugh.*)

Ms. Margaret: Roscoe, Abby show Roscoe his quarters. (*Abby and Roscoe walk away and Ms. Margaret immediately turns to Allison.*)

Ms. Margaret: So Allison you felt the need to have an ally, a partner!

Allison: He was at the diner.

Ms. Margaret: Allison Portwine, it will serve you well to always remember that I am much wiser than my daughter, and you as well. (*She walks inside leaving Allison standing in the doorway.*)

Allison: Hum!! (*As she thinks to herself, " Did I hear a Southern accent and attitude in there somewhere?"*)

LATER THAT NIGHT IN ALLISON'S ROOM

Allison: I don't think your mother is so fond of me.

Abby: Oh she's just that way, very protective of me. She doesn't want to see me get hurt or waste my life or something like that.

Allison: She loves you very much.

Abby: Is it love? Sometimes I feel like she thinks she owes me. Come with me. *(Allison and Abby for the first time go to Abby's room.)* Now, do you see? Identical rooms. My mother promised me when I was a little girl that someday she would marry and I would have a sister. This room is for my sister.

Allison: Marry!!

Abby: Yes, my father died when I was very young. To be honest with you, I really don't remember him at all. Whenever my mother speaks of him, I go along just to appease her. I remember very little about my younger years altogether. I remember having a nanny. A nigra woman. She was quite a sweetheart actually. She would sit me on her lap or hold me and just sing songs. I would lay on her chest and rub her belly. I don't know why, but I loved rubbing her belly.

Allison: These rooms are very special. I should not be here.

Abby: Don't be silly. You are special and so is this room. It's like it has just been waiting for your arrival.

Allison: (*Looking straight into Abby's eye's*) So how many sisters have you tried out?

Abby: (*Disappointment on her face*) Why? That's an insult! I know you don't think I befriended you because I had nothing better to do. And with that attitude and lack of gratitude, you can leave at any time.

Allison: I did not mean to offend you. However, I would like to know just where I stand. What is this all about? Are you trying to fulfill your mother's prophesy while she is trying to fulfill your void? Why am I here?

Abby: And just what are you searching for again? Heaven? How does it make you feel? How long have you been searching?

Allison: Heaven? What heaven?

Abby: (*Beginning to laugh*) Don't be so serious. We stumbled upon each other. Let's just enjoy. Besides, I don't have much more time for this kind of leisure. As I said before, mother has assured me that it's either marriage or college.

Allison: Any prospects/potentials?

Abby: Oh I'm sure with mother's help, I can get into any college of my choosing.

Allison: I meant in the marriage category.

Abby: "Jeremiah Mason". He's studying medicine. He's quite refined and mother says he's a perfect catch.

Allison: And how do you feel about this catch your mother has reeled in for you?

Abby: I'm sure mother knows best.

Allison: With such matters, I think one's heart knows best.

Abby: Such matters?

Allison: Matters of love.

Abby: I mentioned love?

Allison: No, you didn't and that's what bothers me.

Abby: I've never been in love. I don't know if I would recognize love or if love would recognize me.

Allison: So you don't love him?

Abby: (*She escorts Allison to her room*) Oh, by the way, mother's volunteering you to stand in for our pianist. She just delivered her baby boy. She will be out for a while.

Allison: Volunteered? Stand in? Pianist?

WEEKS LATER

Allison commences the congregation with "Til We Meet, Til We Meet, Til We Meet Again"

Allison: (*Head bowed*) God, you really do work miracles and in very mysterious ways. Oh, Heavenly Father, please forgive me my trespasses. And this new life, is it a lie? Is it a sin? (*Allison feels a hand on her shoulder*).

Pastor: We all sin. You've come to the right place to rest your sins. So leave you trespasses right here.

Allison: Thank you pastor. (*She extends her hand in fellowship*)

Pastor: Thank you. You play beautifully.

Allison: Again, thank you.

Pastor: Several members have been requesting the possibly of having you give lessons to some of the children here after receiving such accolades from Ms. Applewhite.

Allison: Oh! Ms. Applewhite and her accolades.

Ms. Margaret: (*Walks up accompanied by Abby and an unfamiliar gentleman*). Pastor, I see you've made Miss Portwine's acquaintance.

Pastor: (*Nods towards Allison*) Ms. Portwine, now it's official.

Gentleman: I'm Mason, Jeremiah Mason. (*The two shake hands*)

Pastor: I was just soliciting Miss Portwine for piano lessons for some of our children.

Abby: Hey! How about we discuss this over my mother's pot roast. Besides I'm sure Allison is quite overwhelmed over all this attention.

The group departs. They all walk outside to find Roscoe waiting for them. Roscoe opens the car door for Ms. Margaret and Allison. Abby departs with Mr. Mason. Roscoe seems puzzled as he watches Allison starring at the young couple as they drive away.

Roscoe: (*Looking into Allison's eyes in the rear view mirror*) Did you find heaven in there or did heaven just drive off? Little girl, don't you go and let heaven take you somewhere else! (*He steps on the gas. Ms. Margaret surprisingly does not utter a word, not even a gesture.*)

Roscoe: (*Looks at Ms. Margaret then Allison. He things to himself, "One thing I know for sure, when white folks is quiet they is thinking, yea thinking.*) Straight to Heaven.

When Roscoe pulls up to the house, the others have already gone inside. He sees the ladies out of the car.

Roscoe: Ms. Margaret, I need to speak with Allison about some work I need to do in her room - some work that was on the list you laid out for me.

Allison: Any work you need to do can be done while I'm at the boutique during the week.

Roscoe: Well, I need to discuss some specifics and details.

Ms. Margaret leaves the two outside, looking at his friend with love in his eyes.

Roscoe: Carrie Jean, my sweet Carrie Jean. (*Allison looks at him very seriously knowing Roscoe would only call her Carrie Jean if something was wrong - and something was wrong. Tears began to well in Roscoe's eyes as he turns his back to Carrie Jean.*)

Roscoe: I cannot look you in the eyes for I know we both will soon be wailing if I do. I don't know what to say!
Carrie Jean: Say it Roscoe! Say it now!

Roscoe: Ms. Wyleen, oh God, Ms. Wyleen, I'm sorry.

Carrie Jean: Momma

Roscoe: I'm so sorry.

Carrie Jean: Momma! Gone? When?

Roscoe: Two weeks ago. They had her home-going service last Sunday. I got the word last night. I couldn't hold it no longer to tell you.

Carrie Jean: I have to go inside now.

She joins the others all laughing and drinking cool beverages. Carrie Jean goes straight to the piano and starts to play. "Amazing grace how sweet the sound" with more passion than ever. Ms. Margaret, with passionate   pain,   walks   over   to   Allison.

Ms. Margaret: (*Puts her hand on Allison's*) You've been playing all morning. Please rest. There comes a time when we all have to take our rest. Rest can be good for the soul. (*Ms. Margaret serves her guest.*)

LATER THAT NIGHT

Allison goes to her room and walks to the far side of her bed.

Allison: God! I'm so sorry Momma! My God, momma! (*The sound of Roscoe stirs at her door.*)

Allison: Roscoe! What are you <u>doing </u>here? How did you get in here?
Saying nothing Roscoe sits on the bed. Allison sits beside him.

Allison: Roscoe we can't do this. We can't be together the way we were back home. Why, now, do you have to be like this?

Roscoe: Like the help?

Allison: Like a brother.

Roscoe: My heart is hurting.

Allison: I don't want to hurt you.

Roscoe: I know you hurting too. That's why I'm here. Here to see bout my Carrie Jean.

Allison: I need to be alone.

Roscoe: Never! Never Alone. *(Allison looks into the eyes of her friend then kisses him on the lips.)*

Allison: It hurts so bad. I know you may not believe me, but I've missed her so much. Every day I have missed her. "Momma"

Roscoe: *(Shushing his friend)* I know you loved momma. I loved her too. Always. (*Embraced, the two lay on the bed and begin to cry as they mourn the one woman they know truly loved them both. They cry and cry in the dark.*)

Allison hears footsteps and quietly walks to the door. She sees the end of a long white night gown and the shadow of someone "a woman" on the wall. She knows there is nothing she could do really. She locks the door, walks back to the bed and lays in the arms of her friend and continues to cry.

Allison has been regularly playing piano at the "family church". A few children from the church and neighborhood have been coming to the house for lessons.

Allison: *(Reads the name of her next student)* Penelope...! I have time for a short break. *(Allison picks up her composition and looks at all the names.)*

Allison: 15 students, I never would have dreamed in my wildest, I would be teaching children to sing and play the piano. God you sure have a way with....things. *(Allison embraces herself and is interrupted by a knock on the door.)*

Allison: Penelope, you are early! *(Opens the door to her surprise...)*

Allison: Mr. Mason!

Jeremiah: Please, it's Jeremy. I think we know each other too well for such formality. And may I call you Ally?

Allison: I prefer Allison. Ally sounds too much like Abby. I don't want you to get confused. And I wouldn't say I know you well at all Jeremiah.

Jeremiah: Please Jeremy! And I think that is something we need to change.

Allison: Changing your name won't be necessary.

Jeremiah: I mean the fact that we don't know each other well. Perhaps we can go into town together sometimes.

Allison: Do you mean myself, Abby and yourself?

Jeremiah: I have known Abby for quite some time and she doesn't show much interest in getting to know me any more than she already has. I think she would rather go away to school in the fall.

Allison: And what was the reason for your stopping by again?

Jeremiah: Oh, I want to let Ms. Margaret know about the new shipment of cars my uncle just got in. You can come by and take a look yourself sometime.

Allison: Penelope should be here soon. (*The front door opens.*)

Roscoe: Allison-Penelope. Mr. Mason I'll show you out.

Jeremiah: I can find my way. *(He walks away then pauses as he watches this vision <u>in white, embrace her pupil</u>)* What beauty!

Easter Sunday, Ms. Margaret, Abby and Allison get out of the new car, the one Roscoe is proudly driving of course. Ms. Margaret and Abby sit together. Allison takes a seat at the piano. Jeremiah Mason is nowhere to be found. There is some singing and much praying. All enjoy Easter service. Afterwards, the ladies receive various compliments and comments on the new car. No one seems to be more proud than Roscoe as he gets out to open the door for each of the ladies, while all eyes are on Allison.

Jeremiah: *(Walks up and closes Ms. Margaret in.)* Ladies, don't forget the social next Friday night. *(Roscoe drives off; Mr. Mason takes account of his toes)*

FRIDAY NIGHT SOCIAL

Roscoe escorts Abby and Allison inside and returns to the car. He sits in style with his cap over his face. Inside, Abby explains that Ms. Applewhite was at home "a bit under the weather". Abby and Allison, no doubt, are the two most beautiful ladies at the party. Abby dressed in emerald and Allison in ruby. Their gowns are magnificent. Mr. Mason walks up, and greets both ladies.

Mr. Mason: (*Being careful to be appropriate extends, his hand to Abby*) May I?

The two go onto the dance floor, Allison begins to mingle with some of the other ladies. A few minutes later Abby and Jeremiah join Allison. Shortly, the music begins again. Jeremiah has not taken his eyes off Allison since they walked in.

Abby: They play so beautifully.

Jeremiah: Oh! Yes they do. (*Abby walks away and joins the company of two handsome gentlemen. They both immediately extend their hand. She dances onto the floor with the lucky guy of her choice*).

Jeremiah: I guess that leaves the two of us. Lucky for me.

Allison: I have to dance with you by default. I'll pass!

Jeremiah: Ally!

Allison: Allison!

Jeremiah: I didn't want to embarrass you. I can see that you are a bit uncomfortable in this place.

Allison: Perhaps, you did not want to disappoint Abby?

Jeremiah: She has been known to cause a scene.

Allison: So you were saving yourself from embarrassment?

Jeremiah: Abby cares for me, but she doesn't love me. She just wants to control me, possess me perhaps.

Allison: And you her?

Jeremiah: I decide who I love.

Allison: And I will never be possessive. Let's dance, I think that's safer than talking.

After dancing for what seems to be for hours, the couple walk into the parlor area for drinks. They sip fine wine and laugh and talk and sip some more. Allison's laugh is chilling. Chilling straight to the bone. So chilling it drew Abby's eyes straight towards her. Disappointed at what she had just seen. She said nothing but hurried out of the room. Allison now notices and looks up to see only the tail end of Abby's gown and a shadow on the wall. Now even more confused, Allison is not sure if the

person outside her door that night was Ms. Margaret or Abby.

Allison realizes she has been left behind. She turns to Jeremiah and they begin to dance. It is obvious by now they're both feeling the same way about each other. Likewise, it seems to be the appropriate thing to do. They kiss and kiss and kiss.

BACK AT THE ESTATE

Ms. Margaret: (*Looking in on her daughter who is fast asleep*) You really don't want him do you? You foolish girl (*walks away*)

Abby: Not by a man who doesn't want me! (*Not asleep at all*)

Roscoe: (*Laying flat on his back in his bed*) Carrie Jean, please forgive me for leaving you behind. Dear Lordy, please keep Carrie Jean safe! Lordy, do you hear me? Safe! Please sir, safe!
Later during the night, Roscoe awakens to the sound of a car door opening and closing. Looking out the window of his quarters, he sees Carrie Jean and Jeremiah. Assured of her safety, he lays down again.

Roscoe: Safe! Thank you Lordy, sir! She safe! Least 'til morning come and she face Ms. Margaret and

Abbigayle Applewhite. She sho' gon' need you some more Lord!

Next morning all sit at the dining table - Ms Margaret, Abby, Allison. There are no questions asked, no explanation given.

(Tap, tap, tap at the door)

Ms. Margaret : So early *(As she opens the front door)*.

Jeremiah: Yes, I'm here for Miss Allison. I will be taking her to my uncle's car lot. She will be needing her own vehicle soon.

Ms. Margaret : Oh! Is that so? And have you been giving her drivers lessons also?

Allison: *(Nervous no doubt)* I've been thinking once Abby leaves for college in the fall, I will need a car of my own to get around. Roscoe's been teaching me to drive.

Abby: *(Finally joins the conversation)* Have you considered new living arrangements? Or will Mr. Mason be assisting you in that area as well?

Ms. Margaret: *(Stands and walks towards the front door)* You two enjoy your car shopping.

Allison and Jeremiah arrive at the car lot. They look at many brand new spit shinny beautiful cars.

Allison: You know, Jeremy, these cars are so fabulous. All of them, but I think I want a pickup.

Jeremiah: A pickup!!

Allison: Yes, a pickup.

Jeremiah: For such a sophisticated and feminine woman such as you?

Allison: There's no sophistication in a pickup? Is that what you are telling me?

Jeremiah: Allison, you will be a sophisticated lady no matter what you are driving or what you are doing for that matter.

The two hand in hand walk inside to ...... they purchase Allison's first automobile. Hot dog!! Shortly, Jeremiah escorts Allison to the driver's side of the beautiful black Chevrolet.

Jeremiah: I can pick up my car later.

After much driving, "joy riding" that is, Allison pulls up to a cabin outside of town. They get out of the car and start walking.

Allison: It's nearly nightfall

Jeremiah: It is so beautiful here at night.

Allison: So is this the place of your many rendezvous?

Jeremiah: *(pulls Allison into his arms)* Allison, you are special to me. My words are not just some cliché'. I am falling in love with you.

Allison: Don't do this.

Jeremiah: It's too late, I have fallen! I love you! *(They begin to kiss. After a sensational kiss, Jeremiah reaches into his pocket and takes out a beautiful locket and puts it around Allison's neck).*

Allison: It's beautiful! *(They begin kissing again and again. They find themselves laying on the ground looking up at the night's blanket of stars.)*

Jeremiah: The glimmer in the stars don't even begin to compare to the beauty in your eyes!! *(Again, kiss, kiss, kiss)*

Later that night, both cars pull up to the estate. Jeremiah gets out to open the door for Allison. Allison and Jeremiah head for the door. To Allison's surprise, she sees Ms. Margaret and Roscoe standing by his quarters arguing! It seems quite intense. She kisses her love good night and goes inside. Later after retiring to her bed, Allison notices the train of a nightgown walking past her door. The light shining through the crack at the bottom of the door reveals a pause. Then lace and footsteps walk away)

SEVERAL WEEKS LATER

Abby is in the parlor with her face in her hand.

Abby: This wasn't supposed to happen

Ms. Margaret: My precious.

Abby: He really doesn't want me.

Ms. Margaret: You <u>really</u> don't want him!!

Abby: Yes! I mean no, not really! But the choice should have been mine.

Ms. Margaret: It's not too late. If he believed you wanted him, that girl wouldn't have a chance.

Abby: I've tried. I made a fool of myself. He refused me. Jeremiah is in love with Allison.

Ms. M: I'm sure it's not really love.

Abby: He is in love with Allison.

Ms. M: Not love

Abby: He has made love to her. The way he looks at her; it's love. He refused to touch me. I waited too late!!! I hate her; no I don't hate Allison. I just hate this; I want him mother.

Ms. M: Then you shall have him. *(Ms. M kisses her daughter)* I will take care of everything, I want you to get packed. You're going to visit your godmother for a few days.

LATER THAT NIGHT

Allison sits in her room. The sound of the door opening startles her since it is without a knock.

Allison: Come in Abby *(To Allison's surprise)*

Ms. M: Hello Allison *(Allison stand as she has never seen Ms. M step into "her" room.)*

Allison: I thought you were Abby.

Ms. M: Abby's out of town, but she'll be back in a few days. I expect you to be gone when she returns.

Allison: Gone? Well, I suppose I could find another place in a few days if you insist I leave your property.

Ms. M: You don't understand, I want you far away from here. Go back to where you came from.

Allison: I don't plan to go anywhere. I love it here. Jeremiah wants me here.

Ms. M: Mr. Mason should be proposing to my Abby, not you!

Allison: But he loves me. We are in love.

Ms. M: Do you think he would love you if he knew?

Allison: Uh!

Ms. M: Yes, nigger! I knew who you were and what you were the minute I laid eyes on you.
Allison, with fear in her eyes, walks towards the door.

Allison: Roscoe! Roscoe!!

Allison: This won't work. Jeremiah loves me. He won't let me go.

Pulling Allison by the arm and throwing her on the bed.

Ms. M: You will leave on your own! Get packing. Carrie Jean Parker!! *(Allison grabs her stomach)*

Allison: No!

Ms. M: You can't be! *(slaps Allison's face)* What do you think the good doctor would do if he knew he had been made a fool of by a nigra? He would probably <u>tar and feather</u> you himself!

Allison: Ok! I'll leave. Just give me a couple of days! *(crying and afraid)*

Ms. M: No! Now! Right now! As a matter of fact, don't bother packing; I'll send your things. I know just where to send them. I want you on the next train out of here. Just think, you almost passed and I would have allowed you to. I would have kept your secret forever if you had not interfered with my daughter's happiness. *(Ms. M tosses two train tickets on the bed)*

Ms. M: Yes, both of you! *(She walks out of the house and drives off in her car)*

Allison continues to cry and is in shock as she hears the car drive away. Allison holds her stomach and looks into the mirror.

Allison: Heaven! Where did you go? Why are you sending me back there? Without momma, there is nothing back there for me. I can't go back there.
Allison rushes out of the house. She goes straight to Roscoe's quarters and knocks on the door.

Allison: Roscoe! Darn you Roscoe!

Roscoe: Allison *(having his daily shave)*

Allison: You mean Carrie Jean, Carrie Jean Parker right?!

Roscoe: Allison? What be the matter?

Allison: You! You Roscoe! I trusted you! I thought you were the one person I could trust in this world.

Roscoe: Oh! Just me Roscoe. You could only just trust me. Not even Mr. who done gone and knocked you up! Yea, Roscoe know 'bout that.

Allison: (*Shocked and angry slaps Roscoe's face, shaving cream splatters*) How dare you?!?! You go sneaking around in cahoots with Ms. M! What did she promise you, huh? You dumb nigger. Well guess what? She is sending both of us niggers packing. (*Allison throws the train passes on the floor.*)

Roscoe: *(With hurt and tears in his eyes)* Allison, No!

Allison: It's Carrie Jean! Or did you forget who I am as well? I suppose you remembered long enough to sell me out!

Roscoe: *(crying)* No Carrie Jean! No! I don't believe in betraying no friend.

Allison: Friend! I've seen how you've been carrying on with her lately.

Roscoe: Carrying on, now just who done went and got a knocked up belly with a white man? Ain't that how nigra women do? Just keep having babies for the white man? Least most of them had no choice. Nobody made you lay down.

Allison: *(begins crying and hitting Roscoe)* No! No! No! We are in love! He loves me! He will still want to marry me when he finds out about our baby.

Roscoe: Where is he? Huh? You don't see him down in no niggers quarters do you?

Allison: *(still hitting Roscoe)* Stop it! Is that it? Stop your jealousy. Is that how she got you on her side?

Roscoe: No, I didn't want her to hurt you. I was always looking out for you. I know these folks will turn on you in a minute. Just like that. *(both sob as they kneel to the floor. Allison knows her friend would never betray her.)*

Allison: *(holding her belly)* What are we going to do now? I can't go back there. You go! Go, Roscoe before we both end up in a bad way!

Roscoe: But I gotta keep taking care of you and the baby. You my family.

Allison: God! We gotta go or we will end up in a mighty bad way! *(The two friends lay in each other's arms crying as they've done so many times before)*

SEVERAL WEEKS LATER

Jeremiah finds himself at the home of Ms. Margaret Applewhite. Ms. M greets Mr. Mason at the door. They walk inside. Obvious to Mr. Mason, many things have changed. Conversation ensues. Apparently, not as expected as expressed by Mr. Mason. Instead there are threats, apologies, and much pleading by Ms. M.

Jeremiah: *(As he storms out of the house and gets into his vehicle)* I am in love with Allison. We love each other. I will go to the end of the world if I have to. I will find Allison.

Ms. M: Abby!!! (*As she rushes to the door, Ms. M and her daughter follow after Jeremiah.*)

Meanwhile, Allison Portwine finds herself on the train. Dajavu in reverse as she reminisces: the good times, the fun times, falling in love. Finding heaven.

Allison: Some people want it all, but I don't want nothing at all if it ain't you baby. If I ain't got you baby, it ain't nothing!

An old pickup pulls up to the familiar worn out shack. Allison gets out and pays the driver.

Allison: Thanks for the lift. (*The man pulls off. Allison coughs as she tries to fan away the dust with her hand. Allison stares. For a moment she feels as though momma is going to walk right up to her. That doesn't happen. She looks to her left. Vivid memories of Carrie Jean and Roscoe playing in the yard play in her mind.*)

Voice: Roscoe, I'm going to get you!!

(*The piano plays a few bars, she walks over to the "big chair" in the corner and sits. Sips some brandy.*)
Allison: "It ain't nothing if I ain't got you".

Allison wakes to the sound of car motors, slamming of car doors and loud voices. She couldn't see anything because it was so dark. She makes her way to the front door which had been left open all this time. Almost blinded by headlights, she could see her friend.

Allison: Roscoe! Roscoe! *(She also sees what appears to be drunken rednecks.)*

Allison: Roscoe!

Roscoe: It's all right Carrie Jean. *(being pushed aside by non other than Bishop.)*

Bishop: What do we have here: *(Staring at Allison's huge belly.)* "Carrie Jean Parker" *(Roscoe makes a move toward his friend but is held back by the bullies.)*

Bishop: *(Pulling at Allison's arm)* I'd say we have some unfinished business.

Allison: *(Holding her pregnant belly)* "God, no" *(pulling away from Bishop she falls to the floor. Now in pain and fear she sees a pool of blood then blacks out).*

Roscoe: *(pulls free, rushes to Carrie Jean)* There is so much blood. She's getting cold! Carrie Jean don't get cold, please don't get cold. *(Roscoe rocks his beloved Carrie in his arms. His outcry goes straight through the roof of the house. So piercing and painful it caused a bold of lightening to crack the sky!)*

Roscoe: NO! NO! NO! NO! NO! UH! UH! Carrie Jean! UH! UH!

Outside was the sound of approaching vehicles. Bishop and his gang meet the "good people".

Bishop: I'm sorry folks, but you don't want to go in there.

Mr. Mason: Excuse me! My fiancé is in there.

Bishop: If you love her, you won't go in there. I'm trying to spare you.

Mr. Mason: What is going on here!?

Bishop: I'm sorry but she's gone.

Mr. Mason: Gone?

Bishop: Dead!! It's horrible, spare yourself; don't go in there.

Mr. Mason: My child!!!!

Bishop: Dead, they're gone sir, I'm sorry sir.

Roscoe: *(Shouting)* Mr. Mason, get back, back. Don't come!!! I want to spare you. She...she went laborin' the baby.

Mr. Mason walks back to his vehicle, gets in and begins to sob.

Mr. Mason: Allison, I am sorry I didn't get to you in time; what happened? What happened? I wanted to take care of you. I love you. I would have kept all your secrets. Why did you come back here? What is this place. My love, please forgive me. *(Knowing there is nothing he can do, Jeremiah drives away.)*

SHORTLY AFTER

Abbigayle and Ms. Margaret r arrive at the "old place". Abby begins to have flashbacks. She recognized this place! She sees a little girl running in this yard. She recognizes this little girl is her!!!

Abby: I know this place! *(of course mother is shocked)*

Mother: But you were so young!!

They are greeted by the men who sincerely want to spare them of such grief.

Man: Allison is dead, she's gone!

Abby: Mother!

Ms. Margaret: It's ok

Abby: Ok? They just said Allison is dead!

Flashes! Flashes!! Abby realizes that all her premonitions were real. She vividly remembers the way she was taken away from her nanny. She remembers falling off the wagon into her nanny's arms. She can hear the voice of nanny screaming, "My baby! My baby!"

Abby: Mother! You're not my mother. Allison was my real sister!! She came here because this was her home and mine!

Ms. M: I have loved you!

Abby: You don't know what love is. That's why you've held on to the name of a dead man who never existed for so many years. Because you know the truth. No one will love the likes of you. You selfish woman!

Ms. M: *(For the first time in her life, slaps the face of Abby)* I dare you! I have put up with your selfishness, your ungratefulness for years. I have tolerated every stray cat, dog, and nigger that you brought in out of the rain.

Abby: Maybe because that's the only way you could come close to having even a taste of heaven!

Abby: Who are you?

Mother: I am your mother! I've always loved you! Raised you!

Abby: And who did my mother have to love after you took me away from her?

Abby: I'm nigra! Are you telling me I'm nigra? Allison's nigra? Who are you?

Mother: I am your mother. You are Abbigayle Applewhite! Look at your skin. No one has ever known or ever has to know that you are nigra, not even Jeremiah. Your skin is white! You've always passed-you're white.

Abby: You're telling me that my whole life has been a complete lie?

Mother: Look at your skin! You are who and what you say you are. *(Ms. M remembers the site of her own mother on her death bed –"Margaret you were the apple of your Father's eye. I should have been and not you." On her death bed she told me I was a nigra child and she was a nigger woman. My own mother! Why did she have to do that to me? Why couldn't she just die and leave me in peace?)*

Abby: I'm nigra. *(Abby gestures to appear as proud as she possibly could)* I am nigra!

She walks back to the car, gets in the back seat with only one word to the chauffeur.

Abby: Drive! *(They drive away.)*

LATER

Roscoe, after pushing Allison's (Carrie Jean) truck into the river and watching it sink, picks up a bag and a stone and returns to Carrie Jean. He places one red rose on her grave site and says...)

Roscoe: Goodbye Allison, "my friend". *(He places the head stone which reads "Allsin")*

Roscoe: My love Carrie Jean, you ain't dead, you are in heaven, right here in my heart."

Roscoe picks up his belongings and walks away. A few moments later, he opens the pile of blankets and places the beautiful man child on the doorsteps.

The voice of Roscoe was so weary as he was relived of the whole experience.

Roscoe: *I have never been able to forget 'bout that day-Ms. Wyleen crying out. The look in that woman's eye was so sad. I felt sad too, having to watch a woman who had been so good to me being treated in such a bad way. The both of us knew if things didn't turn out their way they would have killed the two of us nigras. But, not even that whip could stop Ms. Wyleen from having her say...reliving...as they tore the child from her arms.*

FLASHBACK

Negro Woman: What about when she start having babies-she won't be barren like you!! She will have a manchild. Any manchild come from my blood will be known nigra!! Cause some things you just can't hide. Lease not forever". My beloved daughter, have yourself a manchild.

Roscoe: That's what she told her little girl Sara.

Roscoe: (*with tears in his eye*) I loved Carrie Jean! I just wanted to take care of "my Carrie Jean".

Kay: (*puts her hand on Roscoe's shoulder*) You did good Roscoe. You took real good care of Carrie Jean. No one else could have done better.

Bishops men carry him to their car. Bishop is barely conscious but lucky to be alive after being shot by his own men.

Freddie B: (*obviously in shock*) My God! The plight of such a young woman! My God, the plight of my mother.

Kay: (*Looking at the beautiful rose bush where Carrie Jean/Allison was obviously buried and the stone that reads "Allsin"*) Yes, we have all sinned against one another, God please forgive us of our many trespasses.

Freddie B walks over to his beloved Makayla.

Freddie B: Makayla, thank you. (*The two embrace and just stand still*)

THE END

CONCLUSION

Abbigayle Applewhite left the Chicago area and moved to Charlotte, North Carolina where she met and eventually married George Dandridge, a Bishop in the Methodist Episcopal Church whose father was a direct descendant of Nigeria. They had eight children. All of whom were aware and proud of their multiracial (African, African American, Native American Indian/Irish American and Italian) Heritage.

Freddie B. inherited the estate that belonged to his grandmother, Ms. Wyleen. Now, very wealthy, he was able to spend much more time with Makayla. He finally made that trip to Atlanta.
The last of the Bishops died.

ABOUT THE AUTHOR – *Myra L. Turnage*

For the first 17 years of her life, Myra spent most of her time in rural Mississippi. Both her parents and grandparents were born and raised in a small town less than 50 miles from Memphis. Growing up there, she experienced very little cultural versatility. Racial tension was at a minimum, probably because of segregation. Myra's interaction with people who did not look like her came when she attended High School where competition was more about popularity than race.

Myra attended college at Jackson State University where she began studying towards her nursing degree. She completed her studies at Ole Miss, Home of the Rebels. After graduating and practicing nursing in Jackson for a few months, Myra moved to Atlanta, Ga. In Atlanta, she continued her nursing career. However, her passion for writing, which she has had since grade school, seemed to overtake her interest so she began putting pen to paper. Please enjoy this story about individuals whose lives were worlds apart but were bonded by strength, love and hope.